Advance Praise for Evalu
Teachers: Mission

For anyone who cares about education as a profession and teaching as an avocation, Jim Popham's Evaluating America's Teachers: Mission Possible *will be an important tool in constructing or adapting teacher evaluation systems that are both fair and effective. Popham is softly critical of ineffective practice and common misperceptions but strongly proactive in his belief that this can be done—we can create teacher evaluation systems that are fair and have a positive impact on student learning. I truly feel after reading* Evaluating America's Teachers: Mission Possible *that this task is not only, in Popham's words, a "mission possible," but it is a mission critical for America's schools.*

Tom Foster
Kansas Department of Education, Topeka, Kansas

W. James Popham is my go-to authority as we navigate the exceedingly important, and often confounding, issues surrounding teacher-evaluation policy. Evaluating America's Teachers *demonstrates Dr. Popham's extraordinary depth of understanding, both as a distinguished researcher and former teacher, and his witty and lucid writing style makes it a joy to read. Mandatory reading for educational policymakers.*

As America's educational policymakers wrestle with revamping teacher evaluation systems, decisions are likely to be made that will have real and significant consequences in classrooms—the stakes are high. Every school board member in the country needs a solidly researched, clearly articulated guide to understanding what works and what could go wrong. Dr. Popham's Evaluating America's Teachers *is that guide.*

Nancy J. Budd, Esq.
Member, Hawai'i State Board of Education (SEA and LEA)

In Evaluating America's Teachers, *Jim Popham brings clarity to the critically important and divisive issue of teacher evaluation. Drawing on a deep reservoir of technical knowledge in assessment and evaluation, Dr. Popham uniquely combines expertise, perspective, and wisdom to present an authentic path forward for policymakers, administrators, and teachers to address the evaluation of teachers in ways that honor the work they do with children in classrooms. If we commit to the disciplined thought and action called for in this eminently readable book, America's teachers and children will thrive.*

Dawson Orr, Superintendent
Highland Park School District, Dallas, Texas

Evaluating America's Teachers: Mission Possible *by James Popham is an enlightening description of methods utilized to evaluate teachers, with strengths and weaknesses described for each method. This book provides insight on teacher evaluation not only for teachers, but administrators and policymakers as well. It informs readers of the essentials involved in teacher evaluation.*

Teacher evaluation is an intricate process and requires a variety of types of evidence to truly measure teacher performance with the intent of improving student learning. The reader develops this understanding as a result of reading this book. The book is easily understood and keeps the reader engaged through the use of humor and examples that enhance reader understanding of key concepts. Perhaps most importantly, this book helps put teachers in a better position to understand where evaluation comes from, types of evidence that can be used effectively and in concert with each other, and that rigorous teacher evaluation is appropriate when reliable, valid, and unbiased methods are used. This book will help teachers understand the value of an appropriate and rigorous evaluation.

Hector Ibarra, Middle School Teacher

For over five decades, Professor Popham has provided sound advice to educators and policymakers about the potential and promise of sound assessment practices to increase student learning. Now, Professor Popham has turned his attention to one of the most challenging issues facing education today: the evaluation of teachers. In his thoughtful book, Dr. Popham provides a clear analysis of why this topic is especially important for educators and policymakers today, focusing on recent legislative acts. The focus that Dr. Popham takes in the book is to address the needs, concerns, and potential for achieving valid, fair, and reliable evaluation of teachers while respecting the goal of providing evidence that teachers are providing high-quality education for our children. In the contentious environment where there are so many competing models for evaluating teacher quality (many of which are seriously flawed), it is refreshing (and essential) that strategies are considered that examine the full range of teacher quality (not just test scores on only reading or mathematics) to achieve a fair, valid, and comprehensive look at the quality of teachers. This book does precisely that and should be a "must read" for policymakers, administrators, and teachers.

Barbara Plake, Distinguished Professor Emeritus
Director, Buros Center for Testing, University of Nebraska, Lincoln

As a chief state school officer who is currently working on implementing a statewide teacher evaluation system that is required to meet the Race to the Top and ESEA waiver requirements, this book provided me with the right questions to ask prior to completion of our work. I believe this book will enable readers to turn the subtitle—"Mission Possible?"—from a question into a reality, and with a careful read there will be many moments of laughter also.

Terry Holliday, Commissioner of Education
Kentucky Department of Education, Frankfort, Kentucky

Occasionally a book comes along that captures what needs to be said about an emerging topic. With respect to teacher evaluation and the recent interest in using test scores in that process, Evaluating America's Teachers: Mission Possible? does just that.

Alan Burke, Deputy Superintendent
Olympia, Washington

Popham takes on the most heated controversy in education and calmly presents a fact-based approach to fairly and effectively evaluate teacher performance. Teachers and policymakers ought to thank Jim Popham for showing how to fairly and objectively create better ways to measure teacher performance.

Jack Jennings, Founder and Former President of the Center on Education Policy
Washington, D.C.

The true power of this volume resides in Jim's description of the enormous challenges local and state policymakers and educator face in complying with the demands for rigorous summative teacher evaluation advanced by the federal government. He helps readers see that neither the evaluation expertise nor the assessment literacy or infrastructure needed to meet federal requirements are currently in place at the local level. In an effective and diplomatic manner, Jim points this out and suggests concrete ways these policymakers, along with local school leaders and teachers, can make sure our students are protected from summative teacher-evaluation systems that do more harm than good. No one should make policy at any level or strive to build a defensible teacher evaluation system without studying this book.

Rick Stiggins, Retired Executive Director at Assessment Training Institute
Portland, Oregon

Dr. Popham is a gifted writer who has addressed an important topic in this book. While I do not agree with all his positions, he makes many true and important points in this book. Particularly noteworthy is his point that tests are not validated, inferences are. A measure that may well allow valid inferences about what a student knows may not necessarily be valid in making an inference about teacher effectiveness. I believe that many of those wishing to evaluate teacher effectiveness miss this important point.

William A. Mehrens, Professor Emeritus, Michigan State University
Lansing, Michigan

Evaluating
America's Teachers
Mission Possible?

W. James Popham

CORWIN
A SAGE Company

CORWIN
A SAGE Company

FOR INFORMATION

Corwin
A SAGE Company
2455 Teller Road
Thousand Oaks, California 91320
(800) 233-9936
www.corwin.com

SAGE Publications Ltd.
1 Oliver's Yard
55 City Road
London, EC1Y 1SP
United Kingdom

SAGE Publications India Pvt. Ltd.
B 1/I 1 Mohan Cooperative Industrial Area
Mathura Road, New Delhi 110 044
India

SAGE Publications Asia-Pacific Pte. Ltd.
3 Church Street
#10-04 Samsung Hub
Singapore 049483

Copyright © 2013 by Corwin

Printed in the United States of America

A catalog record of the book is available from the Library of Congress.

ISBN 9781452260853

Acquisitions Editor: Arnis Burvikovs
Associate Editor: Desirée A. Bartlett
Editorial Assistant: Mayan White
Production Editor: Amy Schroller
Copy Editor: Terri Lee Paulsen
Typesetter: Hurix Systems Pvt. Ltd.
Proofreader: Theresa Kay
Indexer: Michael Ferreira
Cover Designer: Michael Dubowe
Permissions Editor: Jennifer Barron

This book is printed on acid-free paper.

Certified Chain of Custody
SUSTAINABLE   Promoting Sustainable Forestry
FORESTRY
INITIATIVE   www.sfiprogram.org
              SFI-01268

SFI label applies to text stock

13 14 15 16 17 10 9 8 7 6 5 4 3 2 1

Contents

Study questions are available at www.Corwin.com/evaluatingamericasteachers.

Preface

I love mysteries. To be more precise, I love reading mystery novels, especially those splashed with enough international espionage to get my patriotic juices flowing. For me, getting immersed in a good mystery constitutes total escape from whatever's then vexing me. Mysteries have always been my never-miss escapist entertainment.

But the book you're about to begin is not intended to entertain you. Instead, I herewith announce that its intentions are (1) to inform and (2) to motivate. Because you, as a potential reader, are the target of this informational and motivational assault, it seems only fair to let you in on what's coming up in the following pages. Accordingly, here's a bare-bones description of what you'll encounter in this mystery-free volume.

The book's focus is *teacher evaluation*. The reason this topic now warrants our attention is easily explainable. Put simply, there is substantially more high-stakes teacher evaluation going on in America these days than has ever taken place in our nation's history—ever. One reason those stakes have become higher is that the real-world consequences for the teachers who are being evaluated are much more significant than in the past. Literally thousands of teachers will soon be finding themselves either fired or placed on a must-improve track that, if unsuccessful, might also lead to a teacher's dismissal.

Perhaps most importantly, however, the consequence of today's intensified teacher evaluation is certain to have a major impact on what goes on in America's schools. And this impact will either be positive or negative. Those who will be most lastingly affected by our current teacher-evaluation jamboree will be, you guessed it, our children. If we evaluate American teachers appropriately, everyone wins—the teachers as well as their students. If we evaluate American teachers inappropriately, however, we will not only see many teachers being unfairly judged, but we'll also witness a definite dip in the quality of our public schools. As a consequence, many more young people will be the recipients of a less effective education. Because a nation's long-term success is closely linked to the adequacy of the education it provides to its youth, teacher evaluation is clearly a topic to which all serious-minded Americans should attend.

Here, then, is a general picture of what's coming up in the pages to follow. For openers, you'll be learning that the attention now being given to teacher evaluation can be traced to two rather recent federal initiatives. You'll learn that powerful federal incentives have inclined all but a few states to refurbish their sometimes decades-old teacher-evaluation procedures. These new teacher-evaluation programs, if they satisfy federal recommendations, can have a beneficial impact on a state's public schools. You'll also discover why, if a state's teacher-evaluation procedures are flawed, too many teachers will be inaccurately evaluated. You'll learn that—because of the diverse and distinctive settings in which each teacher functions—no unbending, one-size-fits-all evaluative process will ever work to accurately appraise different teachers in different contexts.

It will be argued that a defensible determination of a particular teacher's quality must be based on quality-illuminating *evidence* regarding the teacher's instructional skill. Yet, because no single source of evidence, all by itself, is sufficient to accurately determine a teacher's quality, *multiple* kinds of evaluative evidence should always be assembled when appraising any teacher. Teacher evaluators must, thereafter, determine what evaluative weight to give each piece of evidence, and then decide whether any of those weights need to be adjusted because of the particular instructional setting in which a teacher works.

We'll be taking a five-chapter look at the major kinds of quality-illuminating evidence that are potentially usable when evaluating teachers. In those chapters you'll get some guidelines to help you determine how much evaluative influence to give to different kinds of evidence. That is, advice will be supplied regarding how prominently such evidence should be featured when determining a teacher's quality. A recommended process for evaluating teachers will be introduced—a process rooted in evidence-based judgments that are, hopefully, rendered by properly trained teacher evaluators. The book will be wrapped up with suggestions regarding tangible actions that a reader might take to strengthen a teacher-evaluation program.

Realistically, depending on where you reside, you will discover that your potential influence on your state's teacher-evaluation procedures is apt to vary substantially from what might be the case if you lived elsewhere. This is because education officials in many states, even though those states comply with federal guidelines, have adopted new teacher-evaluation procedures often permitting meaningfully different levels of discretionary implementation by local educators. In some states, essentially no modifications of state-dictated teacher-evaluation procedures are permitted. Yet, in other states considerable latitude has been given to a state's school districts—and even to schools within a district, that is, latitude regarding how best to implement a state-determined teacher-appraisal framework.

To make the foregoing overview of what's to be treated a bit more specific, here is a boiled-down description of the focal questions to be addressed in the book's nine chapters:

- What underlies the current furor about teacher evaluation? Moreover, can even well-intentioned, federally reviewed teacher-evaluation systems be ineffectual? (Chapter 1)
- How important, if at all, is human judgment in the evaluation of teachers? (Chapter 2)
- Why should teacher evaluation be based on evidence-illuminated judgments? (Chapter 3)
- What sources of quality-illuminating evidence might be used in a teacher-evaluation program, and how can we determine the evaluative influence assigned to such evidence? (Chapters 4–8)
- How can someone contribute meaningfully to the generation of a worthwhile teacher-evaluation program or to the improvement of a flawed teacher-evaluation program? (Chapter 9)

There it is—a description of what's in store if you give this book a cover-to-cover read. As indicated earlier, the book was written to inform readers about the essentials of teacher evaluation so that, based on such knowledge, at least some readers will be motivated to do something to strengthen any teacher-evaluation program they encounter. There's no mystery about what I want—it is for you to become sufficiently knowledgeable about the pivotal issues associated with teacher evaluation so that, to the degree permitted by your state's teacher-evaluation framework, you can either help shape up a teacher-evaluation program that will benefit teachers and students or, if you encounter a weak teacher-evaluation program, you can quickly recognize its shortcomings and then do something to fix it.

In thinking about the potential readers of this book, it seemed likely that most of them can be grouped into three fairly distinctive categories, namely, educational *policymakers,* educational *administrators,* and *teachers.* In the policymaker group we find elected legislators, members of state and local school boards, as well as regular citizens—particularly parents of school-age children. For administrators, the likely candidates are a district's central-office staff including the superintendent and supporting superintendents, but also those school-site administrators such as a school's principal and assistant principals. Finally, we have teachers themselves who, because they will be the targets of these emerging evaluative systems, should have a special interest in a topic that might well have a substantial impact on their careers and their lives. Given these three audiences, it seemed potentially helpful to conclude each chapter with three brief *Chapter Implications*—one paragraph for each group. Because the significance of a chapter's contents for each of these three groups will often overlap, readers are encouraged—if they wish—to review all three sets of chapter implications. These Chapter Implications are less of a "chapter summary" than my take on what seems particularly pertinent to a given group of readers. As noted earlier, especially for teachers and educational administrators, the degree to which these action implications can be acted on will usually depend on the extent to which a state's teacher-evaluation framework permits local implementation variations.

For those readers who individually or collectively, as part of a book-study group, wish to do some additional thinking about a chapter's contents, a set of per-chapter study questions and other resources are available at the following website: www.Corwin.com/ evaluatingamericasteachers.

In fairness, I should point out, as you will soon realize, I have some personal preferences regarding how teachers ought to be evaluated. As a teacher myself, both in high school and in college, I've been the recipient of many such evaluations. Additionally, I've not only kept abreast of teacher-evaluation research for more than 50 years, but I've intermittently tried to contribute research evidence regarding teacher evaluation. It is not surprising, therefore, that I've arrived at my own views about how best to evaluate teachers. You'll see the sort of teacher-evaluation approach I think makes sense in Chapter 3.

If you turn to the book's front cover, I think this book's subtitle actually represents the biggest challenge for a reader. Consider that subtitle for just a moment: *Mission Possible?* By the time you've finished the book, will you conclude it is possible not only to evaluate the nation's teachers fairly, but also to do so in a way that our emerging teacher-evaluation programs have a positive impact on students' learning? I've already reached my own conclusion about the possibility that *Evaluating America's Teachers* will have a positive impact on education. When you've finished the book, we'll see if you and I agree.

W. J. P.

January 2013

Publisher's Acknowledgments

Corwin would like to thank the following individuals for their editorial insight and guidance:

Don Bartalo, Corwin Author and Instructional Leadership Coach
Rochester, New York

Joe Crawford, Corwin Author and Consultant
Freeport, Illinois

David G. Daniels, Principal
Susquehanna Valley Senior High School
Conklin, New York

Dr. Peter DeWitt, Corwin Author and Principal
Poestenkill Elementary School
Averill Park, New York

Martin Hudacs, Superintendent
Solanco School
Quarryville, Pennsylvania

John Robinson, Corwin Author and Principal
Discovery High School
Newton, North Carolina

Carl J. Weingartner, Corwin Author and Retired Principal
Albuquerque, New Mexico

About the Author

 **W. James Popham** has spent the bulk of his educational career as a teacher. His first teaching assignment, for example, was in a small eastern Oregon high school where he taught English and social studies while serving as yearbook advisor, class sponsor, and unpaid tennis coach. That recompense meshed ideally with the quality of his coaching.

Most of Dr. Popham's teaching career took place at UCLA where, for nearly 30 years, he taught courses in instructional methods for prospective teachers as well as courses in evaluation and measurement for graduate students. At UCLA he won several distinguished teaching awards. In January 2000, he was recognized by *UCLA Today* as one of UCLA's top 20 professors of the 20th century. (He notes that the 20th century was a full-length century, unlike the current abbreviated one.) In 1992, he took early retirement from UCLA upon learning that emeritus professors received free parking.

Because at UCLA he was acutely aware of the perishability of professors who failed to publish, he spent his nonteaching hours affixing words to paper. The result: 30 books, 200 journal articles, 50 research reports, and 175 papers presented before research societies. Although not noted in his official vita, while at UCLA he also authored 1,426 grocery lists.

His most recent books are *Classroom Assessment: What Teachers Need to Know,* 7th ed. (2014) and *Assessment for Educational Leaders* (2006), Allyn & Bacon; *The Truth About Testing* (2001), *Test Better, Teach Better* (2003), *Transformative Assessment* (2008), *Instruction That Measures Up* (2009), and *Transformative Assessment in Action*

(2011), ASCD; *America's "Failing" Schools* (2005), Routledge; *Mastering Assessment* (2012), Pearson; *Unlearned Lessons* (2009), Harvard Education Press; and *Everything School Leaders Need to Know About Assessment* (2010), Corwin. He encourages purchase of these books because he regards their semiannual royalties as psychologically reassuring.

In 1978, Dr. Popham was elected to the presidency of the American Educational Research Association (AERA). He was also the founding editor of *Educational Evaluation and Policy Analysis,* a quarterly journal published by AERA. A Fellow of the Association, he has attended each year's AERA meeting since his first in 1958. He is inordinately compulsive.

In 1968, Dr. Popham established IOX Assessment Associates, an R&D group that formerly created statewide student achievement tests for a dozen states. He has personally passed all of those tests, largely because of his unlimited access to the tests' answer keys.

In 2002 the National Council on Measurement in Education presented him with its Award for Career Contributions to Educational Measurement. In 2006 he was awarded a Certificate of Recognition by the National Association of Test Directors. In 2009 he was appointed to the National Assessment Governing Board by Secretary of Education Arne Duncan. Dr. Popham's complete 48-page, single-spaced vita can be requested. It is really dull reading.

Evaluating
America's Teachers

CHAPTER 1

What Underlies the Tightening of Today's Teacher-Evaluation Programs?

E veryone wants our nation's children to be properly educated. Realistically, who would want anything else? Central to such a universally held hope, of course, is the belief that if students are to be properly educated, they must be taught by competent teachers. That's because skilled teachers typically provide effective instruction to their classes, whereas unskilled teachers usually supply ineffective instruction. Unquestionably, therefore, we want America's students to be taught by top-notch teachers.

Thus, it should come as no surprise that, throughout the years, we have often seen attention given to the issue of how best to evaluate the nation's teachers—particularly to the evaluation of those teachers who staff our public schools. After all, if U.S. taxpayers are footing the bill for public schooling, it is altogether reasonable to expect that those taxpayers would want their tax dollars well spent. So, given the patent importance of teachers in providing the nation's public education, the topic of teacher evaluation has been addressed in this country, off and on, for well over a century. Yet, only in the last few years have we seen a serious nationwide effort to appraise the skills of teachers with genuine rigor.

In years past, the day-to-day evaluation of teachers was typically designed and implemented at the district or school levels rather than at the state or federal levels. Moreover, both district-based and school-based teacher evaluations, at least in most settings, definitely operated under the radar. Because the ingredients of a school district's teacher-evaluation procedures are typically part of the personnel contract worked out between a district's leadership and the organization(s) representing its teachers, the public rarely learns about the innards of such contacts other than, occasionally, being alerted to the presence of atypically high or atypically low teachers' salaries.

One element of these collective bargaining agreements that's rarely aired in public is the personnel-appraisal system to be used when evaluating a district's teachers. Frankly, these contractually defined teacher-appraisal programs have sometimes been structured in such a way that it is nearly impossible to terminate a teacher because of the teacher's ineffectiveness. Understandably, representatives of teachers' unions have sought contractual safeguards in such personnel appraisals so that the union's members cannot be dismissed capriciously. In many contractually defined teacher-appraisal systems, such safeguards abound. Because few teachers in America have ever been discharged for cause, and the vast majority of teachers' evaluations have historically been quite positive, it is not unreasonable to label U.S. teacher evaluation as soft rather than stiff.

The September 2012 Chicago teachers' strike, a labor dispute that cost 350,000 students a week's worth of schooling, triggered national interest in the way teachers are evaluated because one of the most contentious issues hinged on the way teachers were to be evaluated. In reporting the conclusion of the seven-day strike, a Reuters reporter noted that, "in addition to the pay raises, the deal establishes for the first time an evaluation system for teachers that is based in part on student performance on standardized tests" (McCune, 2012).

Until recent years, in fact, the only time most Americans became even mildly aware of teacher evaluation was when newspapers recounted details of a tenured teacher's contested dismissal or, perhaps, when significant awards were given to an extraordinarily skilled teacher. As a rule, if schools and districts have had the good fortune to be led by genuinely capable district-level and school-site administrators, teacher evaluation typically took place off stage, and was usually thought to have been carried out properly.

But those days are definitely over. Teacher evaluation has now scurried onto American education's center stage, and that's why this book has been written. An enterprise of considerable importance—the appraisal of our nation's teachers—that heretofore has received only half-hearted attention, has suddenly grabbed our serious scrutiny. So, let's get underway by identifying the two events that underlie today's intensified focus on teachers.

WHAT UNCLE SAM WANTS

Shortly after the outbreak of World War II, as part of a massive effort to get young men to enlist in America's armed forces, a widely distributed poster was seen throughout the land. It featured a stern, finger-pointing Uncle Sam bedecked in ample red, white, and blue who proclaimed, "Uncle Sam wants you!" The poster conveyed a patently patriotic message that our nation needed defenders. And, as history tells us in that particular instance, Uncle Sam got what Uncle Sam wanted.

Now, it seems, Uncle Sam wants something else. Our federal government wants better public schools and, to make them so, it wants America's public school teachers to be evaluated more appropriately. Today's increasing attention to teacher evaluation in most of our nation's states was spurred directly by two significant federal initiatives. Both of those programs were aimed at comprehensive school improvement, and both of them called for the installation of more rigorous teacher-evaluation programs in a state's schools.

In February 2009 President Obama signed into law the American Recovery and Reinvestment Act that provided $4.35 billion for a competitive grant program, the Race to the Top Fund (RTT), aimed at encouraging and rewarding states (and, later on, school districts) that create the conditions for educational innovation and reform. One key provision of this unprecedented RTT program called for states who wanted to receive a hunk of this federal largesse to establish more rigorous teacher evaluation programs using multiple measures in which evidence of student growth was to play a prominent role.

Two and a half years later, in September 2011, U.S. Secretary of Education Arne Duncan announced a flexibility program that permitted states, if their applications were approved, to obtain a waiver allowing them to make adjustments in what would otherwise be expected of them under provisions of the latest reauthorization of 1965's Elementary and Secondary Education Act (ESEA). The version of ESEA then in place, the No Child Left Behind Act (NCLB), had been signed into law by President George W. Bush in early 2002. The ESEA Flexibility Program, as was true with RTT, reiterated a call for the use of multiple measures in appraising teachers, and stressed again that student growth was to be employed "as a significant factor" in a teacher's evaluation.

Because RTT offered a substantial cash infusion for state coffers, when most states were facing budgetary shortfalls, and because the ESEA Flexibility Program gave state officials a way to avoid pinning "failing" labels on more of their schools and districts, it comes as no surprise that the federal call for improved teacher evaluation was heeded. Indeed, as soon as RTT announcements reached state capitals, political leaders in many states tried to create the conditions that would better position their state to successfully snare these federal grants. Similarly, because NCLB's later years called for ever-increasing improvements in students' test scores, more and more schools were being identified as NCLB-inadequate in most states. States receiving an ESEA flexibility waiver could make adjustments in their test-score expectations that would allow fewer schools to be seen as unsuccessful. Thus, because a precondition for securing such waivers was to install a teacher-evaluation system consonant with what had been set forth in 2009's RTT, even more states found themselves "racing" in 2011, but in this instance the race was to avoid more NCLB sanctions. Quite clearly, Uncle Sam wanted improved teacher evaluations, and he was deftly employing both a carrot and a stick to get what he wanted.

Although the teacher-evaluation specifics endorsed by federal authorities in both of these initiatives are essentially identical, it appears that 2011 ESEA Flexibility Program spells out in more detail what was being sought—probably in response to questions raised by U.S. educators about the teacher-evaluation features recommended in RTT.

A FEDERAL VISION OF TEACHER EVALUATION

Given the catalytic impact of RTT and the ESEA Flexibility Program on states' teacher-evaluation procedures, we need to see precisely what it is that federal officials want from states in an attempt to improve state teacher-evaluation systems. Although most federal guidance documents on this topic refer to "teacher and principal" evaluation/support systems, and although principals' evaluations are a clearly important undertaking, the emphasis in this book will be on *teacher* evaluation, not *principal* evaluation. Thus, it is teacher evaluation that you'll be reading about in the coming pages. Some, but not all, of the conclusions drawn about the appraisal of teachers will, naturally, pertain to principals' evaluation as well. But the serious consideration of how to evaluate school principals is a topic best left for another place and another time.

Here, as spelled out in the ESEA Flexibility Program, is how federal authorities describe what state education agencies (SEAs) and local educational agencies (LEAs) must do with their teacher-evaluation programs in order to successfully obtain flexibility approval:

> To receive this flexibility, an SEA and each LEA must commit to develop, adopt, pilot, and implement, with the involvement of teachers and principals, teacher and principal evaluation and support systems that: (1) will be used for continual improvement of instruction; (2) meaningfully differentiate performance using at least three performance levels; (3) use multiple valid measures in determining performance levels, including as a significant factor data on student growth for all students (including English Learners and students with disabilities), and other measures of professional practice (which may be gathered through multiple formats and sources, such as observations based on rigorous teacher performance standards, teacher portfolios, and student and parent surveys); (4) evaluate teachers and principals on a regular basis; (5) provide clear, timely, and useful feedback, including feedback that identifies needs and guides professional development; and (6) will be used to inform personnel decisions. (*ESEA Flexibility,* U.S. Department of Education, 2011, p. 5)

As subsequent federal documents have elaborated on these six requirements, it is clear that an SEA must first generate the guidelines for a state's teacher-evaluation system, but that LEAs should then create teacher-evaluation systems consistent with their state's guidelines. As district-prescribed renditions of a state's teacher-evaluation process reach a district's individual schools, and move closer to the evaluation of individual teachers, then a *school's* implementation must also be in accord with its district-approved, state-framed program for teacher evaluation. Currently, state-level authorities in different states have delegated varying degrees of allowable customization to LEAs in the implementation of their state's teacher-evaluation framework. Accordingly, it should be expected that in any state where local school districts are allowed to devise many of their own implementation procedures, we will see considerable variation in the final versions of different LEA teacher-evaluation procedures. Federal officials also require that all teachers, principals, and evaluators should be properly trained regarding their roles in any district's evaluation program. Obviously, if these new teacher-evaluation systems are going to work well, and thereby benefit students, all of the individuals who have a hand in the process must carry out their roles with understanding and skill.

Throughout the various federal documents describing the RTT and ESEA flexibility initiatives, it is apparent that those crafting these programs are not only interested in evaluating the nation's teachers, they are also interested in supporting those teachers. Thus, although in the following pages you'll *not* see me adding an "and supporting" phrase onto every reference to the evaluation of teachers, you should recognize that the federal proponents of these programs wish to see programs capable of supplying the needed professional development for those teachers who, based on improved evaluation procedures, have been identified as needing professional assistance.

Even though some teachers complain that their state's emerging teacher-evaluation system is intended solely to identify and eliminate incompetent teachers, a careful reading of documents emerging from RTT and the ESEA Flexibility Program contradict such a conclusion. Peppered throughout the language describing these initiatives is an almost constant commitment to providing requisite professional assistance for those teachers who—based on a carefully fashioned teacher-evaluation process—demonstrably need it.

Because the federal vision of teacher evaluation is spelled out more fully in the 2011 ESEA flexibility initiative, let's consider the sort of teacher evaluation that's being sought in the documents describing that program. First off, the just-cited *ESEA Flexibility* excerpt actually employs inaccurate language when it calls for those who devise teacher-evaluation programs to "use multiple valid measures in determining performance levels." This is because it is not a *measure* that is either valid or invalid. Rather, when using educational measures (that is, when using students' performances on educational assessments), what's at issue is the validity of the *inference* one makes by using a measure. That's right; *tests* are not valid or invalid. Instead, it is a test-based *inference* whose validity is at issue.

So, for example, we might collect quality-illuminating evidence about a teacher by seeing how well the teacher's students perform on a state's annual accountability test. It is not the test itself that is valid or not. Indeed, if we attempted to use that very same accountability test to determine a student's weight or a student's height, our resulting inferences would obviously be inaccurate. Tests allow us to make an inference about a test taker. This inference, depending on the appropriateness of the test as support for the inference being made, may be valid or invalid.

While the "valid measures" quibble in the preceding paragraph may seem somewhat picky, it really relates to an important issue. You see, if we start labeling *tests* as valid, then soon we start ascribing interpretive accuracy to the tests themselves. That's a mistake. Remember, it is human beings who make test-based inferences. And abundant evidence is at hand showing us that human beings can make mistakes—usually every few hours. Thus, we need to be careful that the tests we use in a properly designed teacher-appraisal system do, in fact, contribute to a valid (that is, accurate) inference about a teacher's quality. What we need is for evidence to help illuminate a particular teacher's quality, that is, to assist us in arriving at an accurate determination of the teacher's effectiveness.

We must be wary of relying on any evidence that—when used in nonevaluative contexts—permits valid inferences but—when used to evaluate teachers—may lead to invalid inferences about a teacher's ability. For example, determining a teacher's quality is a fundamentally different game than determining a student's achievement level—as you will see in Chapter 4's treatment of test-measured student growth. Use of multiple measuring devices to secure quality-illuminating evidence regarding a teacher's quality is reasonable—but only if the measuring devices employed will supply us with data from which valid evaluative inferences can be made about a teacher's quality.

The federal insistence on the use of multiple measures represents a wonderful message, namely, that if you set out to get an accurate fix on a teacher's quality, then be sure you assemble a variety of measuring approaches allowing you to arrive at an evaluation that's as accurate as possible. Who can quarrel with such advice? Indeed, among the types of evidence that federal officials identify as possibilities are observations of teachers in action, teacher portfolios, student surveys, and parent surveys. Obviously, the architects of these federal initiatives were urging state education officials to cast a wide net when collecting evidence regarding the competence of their state's teachers.

Perhaps the most attention-arresting feature of the entire teacher-evaluation strategy envisaged by federal officials is the stipulation that, among the evidence sources to be used, data regarding student growth is to be employed "as a significant factor." What federal authorities are displaying is a previously unseen insistence on using students' test scores as a major consideration when evaluating teachers. This feature of these two federal initiatives, more than any other stipulation, has generated substantial angst among state education authorities—not to mention teachers themselves.

In years past, although there have been attempts to incorporate students' accountability-test scores into the appraisal of *schools* and *districts,* rarely have we seen serious efforts to employ those test scores in the appraisal of individual *teachers.* Yet, here we have two federal programs—programs with substantial dividends for states—that say, unequivocally, a state must incorporate students' growth as a *significant* determiner when evaluating its state's teachers. Students' test performances, as never before, are now to become a major consideration when determining a teacher's quality.

The message to state officials is abundantly clear: to hop aboard this federally fostered express, you need to embrace a hard-data strategy for evaluating your state's teachers using students' test-score growth as a significant determiner of those teachers' performance levels. It has become apparent, given the number of states seeking an RTT grant and/or an ESEA flexibility waiver, that this is a price SEA policymakers are willing to pay. Be assured, however, that when a state's leaders agree to employ multiple sources of evaluative evidence, and a significant one of those sources is to be students' assessed achievement growth, this is most definitely "not your father's teacher-evaluation program."

Although federal officials will permit a state to exercise a certain degree of discretion in determining how students' growth will be included as a "significant factor" in the state's teacher-evaluation system, the term "growth" definitively requires the measurement of students' status on at least two occasions. For instance, a teacher might measure students' growth by contrasting students' pretest scores on a teacher-made test at the start of a semester with those students' posttest scores on the same, or a similar, test at the end of a semester. Similarly, teachers could compare students' scores on *this spring's* close-of-school state accountability test with those students' scores on *last spring's* close-of-school state accountability test. But *growth,* as that term is typically understood, requires a determination of students' assessed status on at least two occasions. Some architects of state teacher-evaluation programs are attempting to employ statistical machinations to allow "growth" to be calculated via the administration of only a single test per year. Whether federal reviewers will accept such atypical interpretations of the term "growth" remains to be seen.

Additionally, numerous thorny methodological issues loom large such as how we can accurately account for the instructional impact of students' earlier teachers. To illustrate, if most of Fourth-Grade Teacher A's students were taught about mathematics by a stellar third-grade teacher, but Fourth-Grade Teacher B's students had received their mathematics instruction from a truly weak third-grade teacher, is it really fair to penalize Teacher B when her students don't shine as brightly as Teacher A's students on an end-of-year fourth-grade mathematics test? Teacher A clearly got lucky by having her fourth graders arrive in class with gobs of mathematical moxie, while Teacher B drew a group of fourth graders whose third-grade math experiences may have topped out at $2 + 2 = 4$.

As with many federal statutes and regulations intended to improve our nation's schools, it is impossible to foresee all of the potential problems that may arise when governmental guidelines are applied in the real, day-to-day world of schooling. Although federal documents make clear that "teacher and principal evaluation and support systems" must be developed "with the involvement of teachers and principals," it would be naïve to assume that leaders of teachers' unions will not be wary of what will surely be regarded by some as a more threatening way of evaluating the nation's teachers. Moreover, even if all states do not seek RTT grants or ESEA flexibility waivers, it is obvious that huge numbers of American public school teachers will now be evaluated according to teacher-evaluation procedures that have been influenced, perhaps indirectly, by these recent federal initiatives.

But one thing is clear. Many SEA officials are willing to go to great lengths to do what federal policymakers want. A mid-October

2012 *New York Times* report of a Colorado school district's grappling with the evaluation of its teachers indicated that fully 36 states and the District of Columbia have introduced new teacher-appraisal policies during recent years (Rich, 2012). Some state legislatures have enacted laws explicitly specifying the percentage of a teacher's evaluation that must be dependent on the test performances of a teacher's students. In other states, those percentages have been established by state boards of education. In most cases, the percentage of a teacher's evaluation that must be based on students' test scores are definitely substantial. Here, to illustrate, are several states' decisions regarding the percentage of teachers' evaluation that must come from student growth: Arizona: 33–50%, Colorado: 50%, Florida: 50%, Illinois: 25%, New York: 40%, Ohio: 50%, Pennsylvania: 50%, South Dakota: 50%, Tennessee: 50%, and Washington: 50%. Although these student-growth weights were established in states' quests for RTT funding, similar weights are being chosen by states as they pursue waivers under the ESEA Flexibility Program.

Concerned by the recent rash of legislatively stipulated teacher-evaluation specifics, Hess properly warns us that "well-intentioned legislators too readily replace old credential- and paper-based micromanagement with mandates that rely heavily on still-nascent observational evaluations and student outcome measurements that pose as many questions as answers" (Hess, 2012). And even in states where their department of education staffers, unencumbered by legislative statutes, have formulated their state's teacher-evaluation program, what we see is a great deal of "local invention" taking place as these new programs are being born. Clearly, some of those inventions will need to be improved.

WHAT COULD GO WRONG?

In general, what has been recommended by federal architects makes a great deal of sense. Federal officials have supplied a framework for state-level teacher evaluations that, drawing on both experience and research, points state leaders in sensible directions as states forge new teacher-evaluation programs or refurbish existing programs. Early on in this book, I need to say that the teacher-evaluation strategies promulgated in the RTT and ESEA Flexibility Program are, in my opinion, a substantial improvement over the teacher-evaluation procedures previously used throughout the nation. But, of course, potential problems lurk. Let's look at some.

As I was growing up, one of my grandfather's favorite sayings was, "There's many a slip twixt the cup and the lip." I always liked repeating that particular adage—chiefly because it gave me an opportunity to use the word "twixt," which, otherwise, rarely occurs in human discourse. What my grandfather's adage pointed out, of course, besides indicating that sloppy cup-drinking can be messy, is that even the finest of plans can fail when they're poorly instantiated. (I never heard my grandfather say "instantiated.")

Thus, despite my foregoing applause for the federally endorsed teacher-evaluation systems envisaged by the RTT and ESEA flexibility initiatives, I am nevertheless worried that these federally catalyzed teacher-evaluation programs might end up doing more educational harm than good. My chief concern flows from the certainty that *unsound* teacher-evaluation programs will mistakenly identify the effectiveness of countless teachers—more teachers than we need to mistakenly identify. And, of course, mistakenly evaluated teachers will, both in the short term and in the long term, contribute to a worsened education for many children.

Here's how: *Effective* teachers will be seen as *ineffective,* and will be encouraged to alter their successful instructional activities that, based on a mistaken evaluation, don't seem to be working well. Children taught by these teachers, the teachers who have—as advised—jettisoned effective instructional procedures, will clearly lose out. *Ineffective* teachers, on the other hand, will be seen as *effective,* and thus will escape the need to remedy their less than wonderful instructional procedures. Children taught by those teachers, because they could be better taught, will also lose out. Mistakenly evaluated teachers, the strong ones as well as the weak ones, end up supplying less effective instruction to children than those children deserve.

But if the previously federal vision of teacher evaluation is so praiseworthy, how could a state's teacher-evaluation system go awry—especially if it has been approved by federal reviewers? Sadly, even magnificent frameworks can't save the day if those frameworks have been inadequately implemented. And that's my fear—I worry that a given state's implementation of the federal conception of teacher evaluation will not be as good as the conception that fostered it. In my view, there are four serious implementation mistakes waiting to be made—any one of which, all by itself, could scuttle a state's otherwise wonderful teacher-evaluation system.

So that you can be on watch for these four implementation mistakes, let's explore each of them briefly before wrapping up this chapter. Although each of the four mistakes, if made, can cripple a teacher-evaluation system, none of them needs to be made. And, happily, all of these mistakes, if they have already been made, can be corrected.

Mistake 1: Using Inappropriate Evidence of a Teacher's Quality

Poorly chosen evidence. A state's educational officials, those who attempt to plan and implement a federally spawned teacher-evaluation system, rarely specialize in designing or utilizing the evidence-collection tools needed to make evaluative decisions about teachers. Given the federal advocacy of multiple measures for determining a teacher's effectiveness, it will surely be necessary to employ diverse assessment techniques when collecting quality-illuminating evidence, that is, the data or documentation that helps teacher evaluators get an accurate fix on a given teacher's skill. Among the sorts of evidence-collection instruments that state officials will usually find they'll need are (1) observation instruments to view a teacher's classroom activities, (2) rating forms to collect evidence from the administrators or students who see a teacher in action, and (3) achievement tests such as statewide standardized tests or teacher-made classroom assessments so that we can measure students' knowledge and skills.

Yet, even though a number of state departments of education may have on their staffs a number of assessment specialists (increasingly, these days, this is a small number), in most instances those staff members are not familiar with constructing and using data-gathering tools intended to *evaluate* teachers. When federal officials call for multiple evidence sources, they are clearly asking for creation of multiple sorts of appropriate evidence, not more variations of misleading evidence. But almost all state departments of education, regrettably, possess few experienced teacher evaluators familiar with the sorts of evidence-based evaluative systems called for by the recent federal teacher-evaluation initiatives.

To illustrate, one of the sources of evaluative evidence often employed in the evaluation of teachers is information collected via classroom observations. But carrying out accurate observations regarding what goes on in a teacher's classroom is much more complicated than is usually thought. For example, many state teacher-evaluation systems now incorporate some form of classroom observations in their programs, and have based their approaches on one or more of the widely used classroom-observation systems employed in various parts of the nation. (Two of the most popular of these observation systems will be described in Chapter 5.) But state-decreed modifications in those already established observation protocols can sometimes cause serious damage to the accuracy of the evidence they yield.

Implementation Mistake 1 is, perhaps, the most insidious of the four implementation mistakes we'll be considering. This is because, in many instances, the wrong evidence-collection instruments will actually *look like* the right evidence-collection instruments. As a brief example of this first implementation mistake, let's consider a misstep that's apt to be made in many states, especially because of federal insistence on using evidence of students' growth as a "significant factor" when appraising teachers.

Due to the ready availability of students' scores on a state's annual NCLB-mandated accountability tests, many states will be inclined to use students' year-to-year performances on those accountability tests in order to calculate some sort of "growth indicator" for all teachers whose students complete each year's NCLB tests. However, as will be described in more detail in Chapter 4, in almost all instances there is currently *zero* evidence at hand indicating that these state accountability tests yield data permitting valid inferences about a teacher's instructional quality. That's right; there is no evidence that those tests provide accurate indications of how well a teacher can teach!

Can you see that if the tests being used to measure students' growth do not permit us to make valid inferences about a teacher's instructional effectiveness, then it is absurd to evaluate teachers by using the results of such tests, especially when those results are to be regarded as a significant evaluative factor? Because too many designers of state-level teacher evaluations inaccurately believe that "a test is a test is a test," we are likely to see many states heading up their teacher-evaluation collection of evidence by using students' scores on the wrong kinds of achievement tests. Tests that, based on the performances of a teacher's students, can't demonstrably help us identify a teacher's competence should function as an insignificant rather than significant evaluative factor.

Summing up, then, mistakenly employing incorrect evidence to evaluate teachers is the first, and perhaps most important, implementation mistake likely to be made as states undertake their new teacher-evaluation programs. Because of the convenient availability of students' test scores on states' NCLB accountability tests, many state officials will be inclined to employ such evidence prominently even though the use of many accountability-test scores for a teacher-evaluation function may be unsupported.

Mistake 2: Improperly Weighting Evidence of a Teacher's Quality

So, if Implementation Mistake 1 is, in essence, "using the wrong evidence," what about the weighting of that evidence? Weighting mistakes take place when inappropriate evaluative significance is assigned to different sources of evidence such as (1) students' test performances, (2) administrator ratings of teachers' skills, (3) classroom observations, and (4) parental ratings of their children's teacher. Typically, these weightings of the evaluative importance of various kinds of evidence to be used in teacher evaluation are made at the state level by state authorities—usually in consultation with concerned constituencies such as teachers' unions, parent groups, and so on. Even so, of course, weighting mistakes will be made.

A weighting mistake occurs when a given source of evidence is given either far greater, or far lesser, evaluative importance than it should be given. For example, let's assume that a state's education officials have chosen to use only three sources of teacher-evaluation evidence, namely, students' test scores, administrator ratings, and parental ratings, but have prescribed that the following weights must be used when any teacher in the state is to be evaluated:

- Students' Test Scores = 20%
- Administrator Ratings = 20%
- Parental Ratings = 60%

I am, of course, completely in favor of parents. If there were no parents, we would need no schools. However, I think that determining more than half of a teacher's evaluation by using parental ratings of that teacher is silly. There are no predetermined "appropriate" weights to be assigned to different sources of evidence, of course, but because student-growth data must be given significance according to federal preferences, it seems obvious that evidence of students' growth on suitable tests should be assigned great weight when state architects of a teacher-evaluation framework start doing their framing. In the above illustration, a mere 20% hardly seems "significant."

No officially sanctioned guidelines exist to aid a state's officials as they wrestle with the problem of how much weight to assign to different sorts of evidence. In instances when a state's legislature has already made those weighting decisions, of course, there's no need for further state-stipulated weighting. But in settings where per-evidence weighting decisions must still be made, there are few substitutes for asking concerned constituencies to engage in open deliberations about the pros and cons of assigning weights to different kinds of evidence. Those in charge of these sorts of weighting decisions simply must do the most thoughtful, circumspect job they can in nailing down appropriate evaluative weights.

Let's turn, therefore, to another way to botch up the installation of a teacher-evaluation system—Implementation Mistake 3. This third mistake hinges on the way we should employ our quality-illuminating evidence about teachers once we've collected it. This mistake deals with the possible need to adjust the evaluative weight of the evidence to the particulars of the setting in which a given teacher is working.

Mistake 3: Failing to Adjust the Evaluative Weights of Evidence for a Particular Teacher's Instructional Setting

Particular teachers teach particular students who have been previously taught by particular colleagues in a particular school headed by a particular principal and abetted by particular levels of administrative and parental support. To evaluate different teachers as though they were operating in identical instructional settings is naïve. Yet, it is possible that some state-designed teacher evaluations will be fashioned in such a way that the cookie-cutter categories of evidence bearing on a specific teacher's caliber *must* be given equal weight regardless of the particular setting in which a teacher functions. Failure to take a teacher's instructional setting into consideration when considering quality-illuminating evidence for that teacher, then, constitutes Implementation Mistake 3.

In the following chapter, we'll dig into the issue of making adjustments in evidence-interpretation based on differences in teachers' instructional settings. It would be delightful, of course, if all sorts of teacher-quality evidence could actually be treated in the same way—irrespective of the distinctive instructional setting in which a teacher functions. This would make an evaluator's job far easier. Nonetheless, despite the evaluative ease yielded by a never-need-to-adjust approach to evidence interpretation, by not engaging in at least some thinking about the need for teacher-specific weighting of evidence, we almost always reduce the accuracy of the evaluation we make about a particular teacher.

As an example of the need to make adjustments in the evaluative significance we give certain sorts of evidence, let's suppose that George Jarvis, because of diminishing enrollments in the elementary school at which he formerly taught fifth graders, has been transferred to another elementary school where, once more, he teaches fifth graders. To his delight, he discovers that in his new school the level of parental support for education is amazingly strong—and generally positive. In his former school, with its dwindling enrollments, most parents of the school's students were either disinterested or disgruntled, and they rarely took part in any parental initiatives to bolster what was going on in the school. In George's new school, however, annual parental engagement in various school-support activities hovers near 90% at each grade level. Now, let's suppose that one category of evidence to be mandatorily used in the evaluation of the state's teachers is parental ratings, that is, parents' responses to an anonymously completed rating form to be filled out regarding the instructional quality of their child's teacher. When this rating form was completed by parents last year for George, his ratings were middling or below. This year, in his new school, the anonymous parental ratings for George are fabulous. Clearly, when attaching significance to these parental ratings of a teacher's skill, attention should be given to the nature of the instructional setting in which the particular rated teacher operates. To treat the two sets of parental ratings as though they had been supplied by the same sorts of parents—parents who have the same view of schooling—would be foolish.

As enticing as it might be to assume that all sources of quality-illuminating evidence should be given identical weight across all the diverse settings in which a state's teachers function, to do so would be short-sighted. This, then, is the third implementation mistake likely to ruin a state-structured teacher-evaluation program. If evidence-weighting adjustments are warranted in a particular teacher's situation, such adjustments need to be made. Let's look now at the final implementation mistake.

Mistake 4: Confusing the Roles of Formative and Summative Teacher Evaluation

More than 25 years ago, I wrote an article entitled "The Dysfunctional Marriage of Formative and Summative Teacher Evaluation" (Popham, 1988). As you can probably infer from the title, back then I thought that it was a dumb idea to mix formative and summative teacher evaluation. I still do.

Let's get these two labels properly defined. *Formative teacher evaluation* describes evaluation activities directed toward the improvement of the teacher's ongoing instruction. Formative teacher evaluation is focused on helping teachers become as instructionally effective as they can possibly be. In contrast, *summative teacher evaluation* refers to the appraisal of a teacher in a way that is aimed at making a decision about (1) whether to reward the teacher for atypically fine performance, (2) the teacher's continued employment, or (3) the need to place the teacher on an improve-or-else professional-support program. The distinction between formative and summative evaluation we owe to Michael Scriven, the philosopher and educational evaluator who, as a consequence of the enactment of 1965's ESEA, helped educators draw significant distinctions among several functions of educational evaluation (Scriven, 1967).

In a very meaningful sense, the ultimate aim of both formative and summative teacher evaluation is identical, that is, to provide children with a better education. *Formatively,* we want to improve teachers' instructional prowess so that they can do their most effective job in helping students learn. *Summatively,* we want to identify the exceptional teachers who should be rewarded as well as those teachers who, if they cannot be helped, should be relieved of their teaching responsibilities. (If you prefer, such nonimprovable teachers can be "deselected," a current euphemism for "firing" a teacher.) In all instances, either positive or negative, our actions should be taken to help children learn better. But lauding the two important, distinct missions of formative and summative teacher evaluation is not the same thing as saying they can be conducted at the same time by the same teacher evaluator. They cannot.

I once heard a colleague, Henry Brickell, comment that a truly skilled educational evaluator was a person "who could bite the hand of the person being evaluated while appearing to be only licking it." Yes, teacher evaluators definitely need to possess more than a little hand-licking suave if they are going to be successful. But a teacher evaluator simply swimming in suave cannot *simultaneously* be a summative and a formative evaluator. That's because a teacher who needs to improve must honestly identify those personal deficit areas that need improvement. Weaknesses can't be remedied until they've been identified, and who knows better what teachers' shortcomings are than those teachers themselves? But *if* the teacher is interacting with an evaluator whose mission, even partially, may be to excise that teacher from the teacher's job, do you really think most teachers are going to candidly identify their own perceived shortcomings for such an evaluator? Not a chance!

Accordingly, although federal guidelines make it clear that support should be provided to teachers who need such support, and this means that formative teacher evaluation must be prominently employed as part of a state's overall teacher-evaluation system, this does not indicate that formative and summative teacher evaluation should necessarily be carried out at the same time by using the same evidence-collection procedures or the same teacher evaluators. Individuals who truly believe that a combined formative and summative teacher-evaluation effort can succeed are most likely to have recently arrived from outer space. They simply don't understand human nature.

It is understandable how LEA administrators and teachers might wish to inject into their summatively oriented teacher-evaluation programs serious dollops of formative teacher evaluation. It would be so much less threatening! However, as heart-warming and wonderful as improvement-focused formative teacher evaluation can appear, care must be taken so that its presence does not diminish the accuracy of summative teacher evaluation. Similarly, we dare not let the presence of summative teacher evaluation diminish the potency of formative teacher evaluation—a process from which most teachers and their students benefit substantially. The only way to avoid such contamination is to keep the two enterprises separate.

Remember, most states agreed to a serious quid pro quo when they accepted federal insistence on teacher evaluation that, in its summative aspects, was tough rather than tolerant. When federal officials signify that a state's teacher-evaluation process "will be used to inform personnel decisions," this clearly means that such evaluative systems should definitely have a *summative* function. Lacing a summative teacher-appraisal system with so much formative evaluation that it erodes the system's summative mission, then, constitutes our fourth and final implementation mistake.

The statewide evaluation of teachers has the potential to dramatically enhance or diminish the caliber of a state's public schooling. How teachers are evaluated will most certainly alter how teachers teach. Teachers, as is true with all of us, want to be regarded positively. Who among us relishes an adverse evaluation? Indeed, most teachers will make a serious effort to do what's needed in their classrooms in order to secure a positive appraisal. Consequently, such alterations in teachers' teaching will, just as certainly, influence how well or how poorly a state's students learn.

A teacher-appraisal system that inclines teachers to make good instructional decisions is likely to do just that. Conversely, a state teacher-appraisal system that points teachers in unsound instructional directions will, unfortunately, also do just that. It is for this reason that all of us need to understand enough about what's pivotal in teacher evaluation so that we can spot anything that's deficient, and then set out to improve it.

CHAPTER IMPLICATIONS FOR THREE AUDIENCES

As explained in the preface, each chapter will be wrapped up with three brief, paragraph-long attempts to isolate implications of the chapter's contents for each of the book's likely audiences, namely, (1) educational *policymakers* such as school-board members, legislators, and everyday citizens, especially parents of school-age children; (2) educational *administrators* such as a school district's central-office staff and school-site administrators such as principals and assistant principals; and (3) *teachers,* the individuals who are the focus of today's teacher-appraisal systems. It was pointed out in the preface that, as can be seen, a given chapter's implications for these three audiences will often be more overlapping than distinctive.

Thus, readers are encouraged to consider the chapter implications for all three groups. As always, the nature of a state's teacher-evaluation framework will determine the degree to which actions by any of these three groups are likely to succeed.

For Policymakers: Understanding the origins of a state's new teacher-evaluation procedures, and the potential federal benefits obtained by a state for installing a new teacher-evaluation system, can help disabuse policymakers from believing that a state's new evaluative approach was stimulated exclusively by within-state preferences or was *required* by federal law. Moreover, even though a set of federal suggestions may have been influential in spawning a particular set of teacher-appraisal procedures, the ultimate *legal* responsibility for adopting and implementing those procedures most likely falls to the state itself. Accordingly, policymakers must be especially attentive to the legal defensibility of their state's teacher-evaluation framework, and the manner in which it is implemented locally, in order to forestall or combat litigation associated with teachers' wrongful-dismissal suits.

For Administrators: As is true for educational policymakers, district and school-site administrators need to recognize the nature of the two federal programs leading to any significant alterations in their state's teacher-evaluation programs so as to better understand the particular features of federally advocated teacher-evaluation strategies. The six elements of the two federally endorsed teacher-appraisal programs, for example, will almost always be present in the teacher-evaluation strategies of any states that have sought funds from RTT or requested NCLB relief via the ESEA Flexibility Program. Of particular relevance to district and school-site administrators should be the four implementation mistakes apt to be present in flawed state teacher-evaluation frameworks. Attention to those four potential deficits in a teacher-evaluation program, at the state or local levels, can help an administrator decide how much energy to expend in attempting to improve an unsound teacher-evaluation program.

For Teachers: As the targets of a teacher-evaluation program that is likely to have a profound impact on teachers' careers, it seems only sensible for a teacher to know "where these new personnel-appraisal programs are coming from—and why?" More directly, of course, teachers will want to attend to the implementation of the teacher evaluations that are affecting them, and be ready to raise warranted concerns if, at the state, district, or school levels, any of the four implementation mistakes described in the chapter are being made. For example, if heavy importance is being given to students' performances on state tests for which there is no evidence supporting such an evaluative usage, then teachers might wish to engage in further study of this issue so that, adequately armed with pertinent arguments, they can attempt to persuade educational decision makers that more appropriate evidence should be sought. Similarly, if some districts or state are unwisely attempting to merge the formative and summative roles of teacher evaluation, then this is an issue to bring to the attention of the administrators and/or policymakers charged with carrying out their state's teacher-appraisal process.

CHAPTER 2

Human Judgment

Needed or Not?

How important is human judgment in the appraisal of teachers? That is, when evaluating teachers, is human judgment pivotal, peripheral, or really not needed at all? That's precisely the issue we'll be considering in this chapter because, as you will soon see, when anyone sets out to design a sound teacher-evaluation process, the question of whether to incorporate human judgment in the process will invariably present itself. Indeed, the nature of any teacher-evaluation system will depend heavily on *whether* human judgment is involved and, if so, *how* it is used.

Before addressing this crucial question of whether to include human judgment as we tackle the building of a teacher-education system, however, it is important for you to confront a discouraging reality. Distressingly, no matter how much thought, planning, and even prayer we might devote to devising a foolproof teacher-appraisal program, when appraising teachers' abilities, we will always make mistakes. Teacher evaluators who yearn for an error-free teacher appraisal are destined to be disappointed. Mistakes will, unfortunately, be made.

In the previous chapter, it was pointed out that the different sources of evidence we employ when appraising teachers will vary in their evaluative significance, and so should be individually weighted according to their evaluative persuasiveness. Then, too, there are the particulars associated with a given teacher's instructional setting that may oblige us to decide whether to adjust those previously assigned weights.

In any given instructional setting, it will always be the case that meaningful variations will be present in (1) a teacher's unique personality—stemming from that teacher's idiosyncratic history of life events, (2) the particular students being taught, (3) levels of administrative support and leadership supplied to a teacher, (4) parental support of the teacher's instructional efforts, and (5) the quality of instructional textbooks and other materials. This collection of quality-relevant variables, of course, does not exhaust the ways in which teachers' instructional situations might vary. But, hopefully, you can see how each of these factors—all by itself—might distort teacher-to-teacher comparisons. Distressingly, such potentially confounding variables do not queue up in a single-file, easily isolatable fashion, each begging to be controlled or eliminated. On the contrary, these sorts of confounding factors are tightly tangled in different ways for different teachers. And is it these profoundly particularistic instructional settings that we dare not dodge when setting out to appraise any individual teacher.

By the time we try to sort out and, perhaps, compensate for the significant differences in particular teachers' instructional settings, differences that are more likely to represent a dozen such differences than merely one or two, the likelihood of accurate comparisons among different teachers becomes more and more difficult. A teacher's instructional setting matters—enormously.

As we watch SEA and LEA educational authorities in many states currently setting out to devise brand-new, more demanding teacher-appraisal systems, we need to remind ourselves that attempts to come up with flaw-free teacher evaluation are doomed to fail. And one huge reason for this impossibility flows from the varied instructional settings in which different teachers function. It is simply unrealistic to aim for flawless teacher evaluation. Accordingly, while recognizing that there will be a certain percentage of mistakes made when determining the caliber of individual teachers, what teacher evaluators need to do is make sure that the proportion of misses-to-hits is as small as it can be.

It is the myriad particulars of individual teachers that, even if recognized, make the pursuit of mistake-free teacher evaluation senseless. However, as long as teacher evaluators realize that they are engaged in what will be a sincere, but not impeccable, attempt to appraise teachers, this is a quest well worth undertaking. To the extent that teacher evaluators do as effective a job as they can, then the maximum number of students will benefit from a mistake-minimizing teacher-evaluation process. If we can be fair to teachers, and can improve the quality of schooling they provide, then this is clearly an aspiration to be pursued.

HUMAN JUDGMENT'S ROLE

If the architects of a teacher-evaluation process truly believe their teacher-evaluation procedures can be put into effect without central dependence on human judgment, then they will obviously try to devise an evaluative process that, insofar as possible, is essentially devoid of the need for judgment. Rather than trying to incorporate and *refine* any required human judgments, those who put together an evaluation system may try to dodge such judgments altogether. Designers of judgment-free evaluation systems, because their evaluative procedures will typically be as quantitative and as objective as possible, believe their approaches will be more accurate than will any evaluation strategy involving the often erroneous judgments of human beings. Such judgment-free attempts to evaluate teachers have been characterized as "people proof" (Mead, Rotherham, & Brown, 2012, p. 17). Regrettably, such judgment-free teacher-evaluation systems simply do not work. You need to understand why.

Evaluation Basics

When we evaluate someone, or when we evaluate something, our intention is to determine the quality, that is, the worth, of the person or thing being evaluated. Invariably, whatever is evaluated is being appraised regarding its goodness or badness in relation to a particular function. (Although some writers draw a distinction between "evaluation" and "appraisal," I see little difference between those two labels and will, therefore, use them interchangeably.)

When we evaluate things, such as a laptop computer, we always do so in relation to our intended use of the thing that's being appraised. For example, only an oaf would evaluate a laptop computer based on how well it keeps one's lap warm.

People, too, are evaluated in relation to particular functions. When evaluating workers, that is, when we are engaged in *personnel evaluation,* we always arrive at determinations of a person's quality by employing *evaluative criteria.* An evaluative criterion is simply a factor that's being employed to arrive at a conclusion about the quality of whoever is being evaluated. When appraising an opera singer, for example, an evaluative criterion might be the singer's vocal range, that is, the difference between the highest and lowest notes the singer can reach. We arrive at determinations of a worker's quality by relying on one or more such evaluative criteria.

In order to see how a person stacks up against a particular evaluative criterion, we need to rely on *evidence*—evidence that's indicative of the person's evaluative-criterion status. Putting it differently, we need quality-illuminating evidence to help us decide how to appraise the individual being evaluated in relation to the particular evaluative criterion (or criteria) chosen by the personnel evaluator. It is only when we can rely on actual quality-illuminating evidence indicating how well a person satisfies a specific evaluative criterion that the evaluative criterion becomes truly useful in carrying out the appraisal of a worker's quality.

The evidence we select to indicate a person's status with respect to a particular evaluative criterion, then, spells out what the criterion actually signifies. Another way to put it is that we *operationalize* the evaluative criterion, that is, we give the criterion operational meaning by showing how we intend to represent it. Such evidence, then, illuminates an evaluated individual's quality with respect to the evaluative criterion involved.

Perhaps you can think of workers for whom a solo evaluative criterion, represented by only one source of evidence, accounts exclusively for the evaluative conclusion reached whenever such persons are appraised. In the real world of work, we find relatively few

---

KEY PERSONNEL EVALUATION LINGO

Because of the need for clarity when evaluating teachers, the following four definitions should be understood:

- **Evaluation:** Determining the worth of a person, process, or performance.
- **An Evaluative Criterion:** A factor employed when evaluating a worker's quality in relation to a specific work-related function. A worker's quality can be evaluated using one evaluative criterion or multiple evaluative criteria.
- **Evidence:** The data or documentation chosen to give operational meaning to an evaluative criterion, that is, to illuminate a worker's quality with respect to a particular evaluative criterion.
- **Evidence Sources:** The eligible kinds of documentation or data that can be employed to ascertain an individual's quality regarding a particular evaluative criterion.

of these solo evaluative criterion plus solo evidence-category evaluations. You will more frequently find that multiple evaluative criteria or, perhaps, multiple sources of evidence are necessary to evaluate a worker's quality. Let's look, now, at an instance in which a worker is appraised using only one evaluative criterion, but multiple evidence categories are employed to represent that evaluative criterion.

As you've seen, those who design the key features of any sort of personnel-evaluation system are the determiners of how such worker appraisals will turn out. This is primarily attributable to the decisions those designers make regarding which evaluative criteria and which evidence sources will be employed when appraising personnel. The appraisal of people in any personnel-evaluation system always boils down to the evaluative criteria chosen and the categories of evidence employed.

To illustrate how to evaluate a worker by using a single evaluative criterion, but multiple evidence sources, let's consider a professional, namely, a *physician.* When evaluating physicians, you can quickly see that one pivotal choice facing a personnel evaluator is whether to devise a general-purpose evaluation system covering physicians of every stripe, or a specialization-distinct evaluation leading to at least some difference when appraising physicians who possess different specializations, for instance, dermatologists, neurologists, or oncologists. An evaluator's choice between specialty-distinct or general-purpose personnel evaluation almost always depends on the degree to which the specializations involved are so fundamentally divergent that any attempt to evaluate all of them using a single approach would be misleading. To the extent that the dominant tasks of the specialists are essentially similar, however, a one-size-fits-all approach to personnel evaluation might well be the way to go.

To clarify this example, we can gain some insights from an acknowledged specialist in evaluating physicians—the late film star Cary Grant. In one of Cary Grant's most memorable but rarely reprised films, *People Will Talk,* Grant plays the role of a gifted physician, Dr. Praetorius, who employs a variety of decidedly unconventional techniques to improve his patients' health. In this film, when his healing techniques are questioned, Grant often declares that the *only* reason a doctor exists is "to make sick people well." And there it is, if we concur with Cary Grant's analysis, we have a solo evaluative criterion sitting there all by itself, a potent factor by which we could evaluate all physicians. For purposes of this illustration, let's refer to this "making-sick-people-well" evaluative criterion as *wellness restoration.*

Interestingly, even though we might choose to build a physician-evaluation system that's centered solely on our wellness-restoration criterion, we could almost certainly employ different kinds of evidence when determining the degree to which a physician stacks up against such an evaluative criterion. When gauging how well a physician satisfies our wellness-restoration evaluative criterion, we could arrive at several legitimate indicators (that is, illuminators) of the degree to which a physician had satisfied the single evaluative criterion of wellness restoration.

And, of course, we might choose to vary these evidence categories according to different physicians' specialties so that the evidence sources chosen for our solo evaluative criterion (wellness restoration) meshed more appropriately with a given specialization's distinctive requirements. Clearly, the designers of personnel evaluations must make a number of important choices when setting up their evaluation strategies. This point was surely understood by Cary Grant.

What About the Evaluation of Teachers?

As teacher evaluators think seriously about the best way to evaluate teachers, what configuration of evaluative criteria and what sorts of evidence to represent those criteria will be most appropriate? This is really the point at which teacher evaluators determine the essential nature of their personnel evaluation strategy—and these strategy-shaping choices about evaluative criteria and evidence sources will surely undergird any plan to evaluate the quality of teachers.

As indicated in Chapter 1, I've been jousting with teacher evaluation for more than a half century and have often been on the losing end of those scuffles. Yet, we can always learn from losing, and I'd like to put forth my current teacher-evaluation recommendations for your consideration. I will certainly understand if you do not subscribe to my position on this issue. But, even if you disagree with me, please realize that the choices made about evaluative criteria and evidence sources will make, by far, the most difference in the way teacher evaluators try to appraise teachers. Here, then, is what I'd recommend to those who are putting together a teacher-evaluation system.

I think that the single evaluative criterion by which teachers should be evaluated is a teacher's *instructional ability*. Yes, I believe that the dominant factor to be employed in appraising a teacher should be a teacher's effectiveness in promoting worthwhile learning in students. Yet, because various kinds of relevant evidence illuminating a teacher's instructional ability can be collected, such as students' test scores or classroom observation data, this solo evaluative criterion should be operationalized via multiple evidence sources.

It should be apparent to you that, if a teacher-evaluation system were to be designed around a single evaluative criterion, but multiple evidence sources representing that criterion, then such an approach to teacher evaluation would most certainly call for substantial reliance on human judgment. Here's why.

JUDGMENT-REQUISITE CHOICES

The following are the tasks during which teacher evaluators will need to summon their best judgment-making skills to arrive at sound conclusions about how a teacher-appraisal program ought to function:

- Selecting the evaluative criterion (or criteria) that will govern the evaluation;
- Choosing the evidence sources to illuminate each criterion chosen;
- Weighting the selected evidence sources;
- Adjusting, if needed, evidence weights according to the particulars of a teacher's instructional setting; and
- Coalescing the collection of weighted evidence.

These judgment-requiring tasks can be made by different teacher evaluators, ranging all the way from—at one extreme—a solo school principal functioning in isolation, all the way up to—at the other extreme—carefully selected review panels. Whether teacher evaluators are principals or review panels, those evaluators should all have been carefully trained for their important tasks. Ideally, teacher evaluators will also have been certificated via some sort of performance tasks for their responsibilities—but today's dearth of discretionary financial resources for such certification-type endeavors makes this ideal rarely implementable.

The question posed at the outset of this chapter was whether, for teacher evaluation to be fair and sufficiently accurate, human judgment is really requisite. I hope you now agree with me that it most definitely is.

CHAPTER IMPLICATIONS FOR THREE AUDIENCES

For Policymakers: It is not uncommon for educational policymakers to take positions calling for the promotion of a particular outcome, such as the reduction of achievement gaps between majority and minority students, then assume that designated educators and their support personnel will be able to straightforwardly accomplish this policy-dictated outcome. But a key message for policymakers found in this chapter is that the evaluation of teachers is far more perplexing than is typically thought, and it must inevitably depend on the exercise of considerable human judgment on the part of those carrying out the evaluations. Policymakers who believe that mistake-free teacher evaluation is attainable are apt to be disappointed by this chapter's somber message. Hopefully, educational policymakers will recognize that, despite teacher evaluation's challenges, reliance on human judgment offers the best route to the most fair and accurate appraisal of teachers.

For Administrators: Clearly, the degree to which district and school-site administrators are able to adopt and refine the kinds of evaluative judgments called for in this chapter will depend directly on the extent to which a particular state's framework for teacher evaluation allows for district or school variations in such evaluative procedures. If a state's framework represents a "no-variations-permitted" approach, then administrators must hope that the evidence sources selected, and the evaluative weights they have been assigned, are sufficiently reasonable. Otherwise, educational administrators should seek modifications, perhaps collectively, in the way a state's teacher-evaluation procedures are supposed to operate. However, if a state framework permits district and school administrators to exercise some degree of discretion in determining a teacher's quality, then those administrators should strive to make the training of all teacher evaluators as potent as possible. The teacher-evaluation strategy endorsed by the federal government is quite different than the teacher-evaluation approaches in place that most of today's educational administrators have experienced during their careers.

For Teachers: Because teacher-evaluation systems in which human judgment plays a prominent role is apt to permit more teacher-specific, tailored appraisals of a given teacher's quality, teachers should recognize that in most instances a judgmentally based approach to teacher evaluation will be more accurate than will judgment-free evaluation systems. Nonetheless, teachers need to recognize that all attempts to evaluate teachers, no matter how well intentioned or properly implemented, will lead to a certain proportion of mistakes. The enormous complexity of the instructional process simply makes it impossible to avoid evaluative mistakes. Accordingly, the more knowledgeable that teachers can become about the innards of the teacher-evaluation system being used to appraise them, the better positioned those teachers will be in successfully combating any inaccurate evaluations.

CHAPTER 3

Defensible Teacher Evaluation

I don't know about you, but I have always reacted positively to the formal documents supplied by legislative committees or advocacy groups in which a string of "Whereas" assertions (with the *Whereas* usually being italicized) is followed by a "Therefore . . ." At that point in these sorts of analyses, the group's recommendation or its advocated course of action is wheeled into view. Such resolutions, for example, might endorse the enactment of a new law, urge the rescinding of a current law, or demand the recall of an elected official. The focus of these analyses can, clearly, be diverse. Interestingly, the teacher-evaluation position that's going to be advocated in this chapter can be straightforwardly presented in what I will, hereafter, refer to as a "whereas-based analysis."

THE WONDERS OF WHEREAS

What's so special about these analyses is that, before getting around to their actual recommendation, the writers of such documents usually lay out a succinct, point-by-point argument regarding why it is that someone who reads the analysis should endorse whatever's about to be advocated, that is, whatever comes immediately after the *Therefore*. Although one might not agree with each of the document's whereas assertions, at least there is little doubt about the specific reasons a group is pushing for a particular course of action. Typically, a whereas-based analysis provides an easily followed logic trail featuring a series of crisply stated and often compelling reasons. Such analyses usually provide rationales that are both succinct and persuasive.

Soon, a whereas-based analysis in support of *weighted-evidence judgmental evaluation of teachers* will be presented for your review. Hopefully, that analysis will be persuasive.

In the first two chapters of this book, an attempt was made to identify why it is that so much attention is currently being lavished on teacher evaluation (in Chapter 1) and why it is that well-conceived teacher evaluations must rely heavily on human judgment (in Chapter 2). It is time, now, for us to look at the chief features of a teacher-appraisal strategy designed to dodge many of the more serious mistakes likely to be made by the designers of state-level teacher evaluations.

In a few pages, you will find a description of the key steps involved when teachers are appraised via a weighted-evidence judgmental approach. You'll also see who the teacher evaluators might be if such an evaluation approach were adopted. But, first, we need to consider *why* it is that someone would ever want to adopt a weighted-evidence judgment system when evaluating teachers. Indeed, what makes a weighted-evidence judgmental strategy for evaluating teachers any better than the numerous teacher-evaluation models that seem to be springing up all over the nation?

As suggested at the outset of this chapter, one of the most efficient ways of laying out a rationale advocating someone's adoption of a particular course of action is by employing a point-by-point whereas-based analysis. Accordingly, presented below is such a rationale supporting the use of weighted-evidence judgment when evaluating teachers. At the conclusion of the following analysis, a description will then be supplied regarding what a weighted-evidence judgmental appraisal of teachers actually looks like. Before getting to that description, however, please give careful thought to *each* of the points forming the following rationale for the evaluative use of weighted-evidence judgment.

WHY USE A WEIGHTED-EVIDENCE JUDGMENTAL APPROACH TO TEACHER EVALUATION?

- *Whereas* unsound teacher-appraisal systems, because they inaccurately evaluate more teachers than is necessary, will have a profoundly harmful effect on the education of our nation's children; and

- *Whereas* both research evidence and common sense indicate that multiple, not single, sources of evidence should be employed when evaluating a teacher; and
- *Whereas* significant variations exist not only in the quality of much teacher-evaluation evidence, but also in its relative importance when appraising a specific teacher, the evaluative weight of all teacher-evaluation evidence must be judged by itself and when applied in a particular teacher's instructional setting;
- *Therefore,* teacher-appraisal systems should be based on weighted-evidence judgment in which teacher evaluators initially select and weight multiple teacher-quality evidence sources, then determine whether to adjust those weights because of a teacher's distinctive instructional setting and, finally, arrive at a coalesced judgment regarding a teacher's quality.

As you can see from this analysis, its three supporting arguments are that (1) poor teacher-evaluation systems harm children, (2) more than one source of evidence should be used to evaluate a teacher, and (3) the evaluative weight of different evidence sources must be determined both separately and when applied in the specific setting where a teacher works. Let's see, now, how weighted-evidence judgment would actually operate.

A WEIGHTED-EVIDENCE JUDGMENT EVALUATIVE STRATEGY

The heart of a weighted-evidence judgmental approach to the evaluation of any worker, whether they're teachers or taxidermists, involves someone's judgmentally weighing the significance (that is, the evaluative influence) of whatever separate sources of evidence bear on the quality of that worker. Next, judgments must be made about whether to adjust those evidence weights when applied to a given worker. Lastly, an overall judgment of a worker's quality is made based on the evidence using adjusted or unadjusted weights.

But what evidence? That is, what evidence will teacher evaluators be collecting and weighing? It is impossible to weight the importance of evidence unless we know what sorts of evidence we'll be employing. As you saw in Chapter 2, one major determiner in how we tackle any sort of personnel evaluation is the nature of the *evaluative criteria* we use as the basis of the evaluation. Not surprisingly, that's where we get underway in carrying out a weighted-evidence judgmental approach to teacher evaluation.

Actually, the weighted-evidence judgmental evaluation of teachers consists of a five-step enterprise. First, we choose one or more evaluative criteria on which to base our evaluation. Second, we decide on the sources of evidence we will employ to reach a determination about a teacher's quality. Then, once the evidence sources have been identified, we can weight their evaluative importance, so the third step in this process is to determine, separately, the *evidential weight,* that is, the evaluative influence, of each source of evidence we've chosen. In Step 4, we must decide whether to make any adjustments in the weight of each previously weighted, separate evidence source so that in Step 5 we can arrive at a coalesced judgment about a particular teacher's quality based on the assembled evidence. This five-step process is represented graphically in Figure 3.1.

Clearly, the way that a state's officials or a school district's administrators choose to carry out this judgmentally based form of teacher evaluation will depend on a host of particulars, not the least of which are the financial resources available and the personnel resources at hand who can be drawn on to carry out the approach. In addition, substantial differences exist in the levels of LEA autonomy

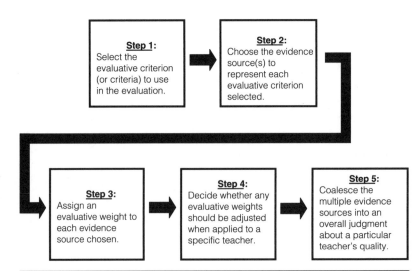

Figure 3.1   Five Steps in Weighted-Evidence Judgmental Evaluation of Teachers

permitted by different SEAs, that is, in the ways local education agencies can set up and carry out their district's teacher evaluations.

The implementation permutations for installing a weighted-evidence judgmental approach to teacher evaluation are, almost literally, infinite. Accordingly, it would be presumptuous to spell out precisely how this evaluative approach should be brought to life in a given state or in a particular school district. There are far too many "it depends" choice-points in a specific setting for anyone to suggest that "this is definitely how it ought to be done." What's important, when considering how a weighted-evidence judgment approach to teacher evaluation might be installed, is for those in charge to grasp the nature of this strategy, and then implement it by drawing on whatever people and dollars are available so it has a reasonable chance to work well. With this in mind, let's look at this teacher-evaluation strategy's five steps.

Step 1: Selecting the Evaluative Criterion/Criteria for the Evaluation

Step 1 in weighted-evidence judgment involves the single, most important decision to be made as we evaluate teachers. This is because in Step 1 the evaluative criteria for determining a teacher's quality are chosen. These evaluative criteria, as indicated in Chapter 2, are the factors we will rely on when concluding how terrific or how terrible a specific teacher is. All the evidence we collect to evaluate a teacher, and all the prioritizing of such evidence that we carry out, will be a waste if, from the get-go, we have chosen the wrong criteria on which to base our teacher-evaluation process. Typically, a state's evaluative criteria for use in such significant formulations as a statewide teacher-evaluation framework will be made thoughtfully and deliberately after seeking the advice of relevant constituencies.

As suggested in Chapter 2, some teacher-evaluation procedures are based on only one evaluative criterion; some are based on multiple evaluative criteria. In certain teacher-appraisal approaches, for example, teachers are evaluated on the basis of their (1) teaching abilities, (2) professional development activities, (3) participation in a school's extracurricular endeavors, and (4) relationships with parents and other members of the community. Such a teacher-appraisal strategy, revolving around these four evaluative criteria—all of which must be represented by one or more evidence sources—would be meaningfully different than a teacher-evaluation program centered on a single evaluative criterion.

As indicated previously, were I to be involved in designing a weighted-evidence judgmental evaluation of teachers, I'd push hard for the adoption of a solitary evaluative criterion, namely, a teacher's *instructional ability*. This is because I think the significance of a teacher's instructional ability dramatically out-distances all other evaluative criteria that might be employed when appraising a teacher. Other evaluators, of course, might prefer to use a different criterion or, perhaps, might choose to employ completely different evaluative criteria when appraising a teacher.

The selection of Step 1's evaluative criteria, of course, depends most directly on *judgment*. Indeed, in the teacher-evaluation approach recommended herein, time and time again there will be the need for human judgment. The more carefully those judgments are rendered, the more likely it is that the resulting judgments will be sound. But, more explicitly, how does human judgment actually take place during this first step of weighted-evidence judgment? Well, to the extent possible, all concerned clienteles, that is, all those who have a serious stake in the quality of the teachers who are to be evaluated, should be given an opportunity to participate in deliberations about the chief factor (or factors) on which the evaluation of those teachers should be based.

In almost every decision-making arena, we find two sets of actors: the decision makers and the decision advisors. To illustrate, at the state level, the decision maker might be a governor or a state superintendent of schools. Perhaps a state board of education's members function as the advisors to the ultimate decision maker. At the district level, the decision makers might be the elected members of the school board, while the advisors might be a specially convened group of citizens who have been asked to give their recommendations to the district school board. When identifying the evaluative criterion (or criteria) upon which to base a teacher evaluation, any astute decision maker will solicit the counsel of an in-place or specifically appointed group of decision advisors so that, insofar as is possible, the voices of those most concerned with the evaluation of teachers will have been heard. And without argument, of course, leaders of any in-place teachers' organization should always be given an opportunity to register their views about the nature of an emerging teacher-appraisal program. Teachers' unions, clearly, have a huge stake in how the teacher-evaluation process operates.

Once the single or multiple evaluative criteria have been chosen during Step 1, then those in charge of the evaluation must once more rely on human judgment as they choose the evidence sources they believe will appropriately represent each of Step 1's evaluative criteria. Such evidence selection takes place during Step 2.

Step 2: Choosing Evidence Sources

As you have already seen, a dominant theme pervading this approach to teacher evaluation is its frequent reliance on human judgment. A second, equally important focus is a preoccupation with the evidence to be used when evaluating a teacher. This judgmental theme and the importance of evidence are clearly evident in Step 2 when those who design the evaluation must judgmentally determine the specific sources of evidence to employ when applying the evaluation's evaluative criteria to judge teachers. As was true with the selection of the evaluative criterion on which to base a state's teacher-evaluation framework, the selection of evidence is usually state determined.

An evaluative criterion that's not operationalized by any kind of evidence turns out to be little more than an empty label. Evaluative criteria become meaningful only when teacher evaluators signify how a teacher's status with respect to a given evaluative criterion will be ascertained. An evaluative criterion that's appropriately represented (operationalized) by one or more sorts of evidence should play a key role in appraising a teacher's ability. On the other hand, an inappropriate choice of evidence to represent an evaluative criterion will almost certainly lead to flawed judgments about a teacher's quality. Clearly, the evidence-selection activities of Step 2 are pivotal if a weighted-evidence judgmental strategy is going to work properly.

For clarity's sake, in this description of Step 2, only a single evaluative criterion will be employed to illustrate how the selection of evidence sources takes place, namely, a teacher's *instructional ability.* During this step in the evaluation process, teacher evaluators identify the evidence source(s) they have decided will be indicative of a teacher's instructional ability.

As suggested back in Chapter 1, the history of educational research is replete with numerous investigations designed to determine a teacher's merit. Because of those sometimes unsuccessful investigations, we now possess substantial experience in having experimented with different sorts of evidence when attempting to evaluate teachers. For example, in years past we have seen researchers often employing the following evidence sources to reflect a teacher's instructional ability: (1) students' test performances, (2) classroom observations of teachers in action, and (3) ratings of teachers' effectiveness supplied by administrators or, sometimes, by students. Also employed, to a lesser extent, have been other sorts of evidence sources such as the nature of teachers' lesson plans or what's emphasized in teacher-made classroom assessments. Clearly, a number of possibilities exist when we consider ways in which we can conceivably get an accurate fix on a teacher's instructional ability.

In general, if the necessary personnel and other costs are within reason, then it seems sensible to represent a given evaluative criterion with multiple evidence sources rather than only one. That is, here is one of those rare instances where "more" actually turns out to be better than "less." Several sources of evidence permit a sort of "confirmation by triangulation strategy," that is, the use of certain evidence sources to confirm or discredit other evidence sources. This sort of triangulation would be impossible if only a single source of evidence were available.

A key task in Step 2 is to identify all of the quality-determining sorts of evidence that might, without Herculean effort, be rounded up for use in the evaluation of teachers. If the evidence-gathering procedures being utilized in such a strategy turn out to be too costly, too impractical, or too complicated, then such pie-in-the-sky advocacy will quite sensibly be disregarded by educational decision makers.

In our current example, where only a single evaluative criterion (instructional ability) was chosen, let's assume that—after careful judgment—the architects of a teacher-evaluation program have decided to operationalize instructional ability by relying on three specific sources of evidence, namely, (1) *students' growth* as reflected by changes in the scores of a teacher's students on the current end-of-year statewide accountability tests and those students' scores on previously administered versions of these tests; (2) *classroom observations* collected by trained observers who make between six and eight 40-minute, unannounced visits to a teacher's class each school year; and (3) *student ratings* of a teacher's instructional skill as collected three times a year via brief, anonymously completed rating forms.

Assuming that judgmental attention has been given to both the persuasiveness and the practicality of our three chosen evidence sources, then the selection of those three kinds of evidence would represent a wrap-up of what's called for by this second step of our five-step evaluation process.

Step 3: Weighting the Evaluative Influence of Each Evidence Source

The third major task to accomplish when implementing weighted-evidence judgment calls for the *weighting* of each evidence source chosen. That is, for all the evidence sources that have been selected to represent the already-chosen evaluative criterion/criteria, we must now make judgments regarding how much evaluative weight we should give to each of those sources. These judgments regarding an evidence source's appropriate weight are not made in the abstract, such as would be seen when we might contrast the evaluative dividends of students' test scores *in general* with the evaluative dividends of classroom-observation data *in general*. Rather than focusing on *categories* of evidence such as students' test scores or administrative ratings, we need to make our weighting decisions about the *specific* data or documentation that will be available in a particular instance. Typically, the necessary weightings are assigned based on some sort of straightforward numerical point system such as 10 points, 50 points, or 100 points.

To illustrate, suppose that one potential evidence source consists of pretest-to-posttest evidence of students' growth based on the use of teacher-made, teacher-administered tests. Suppose, further, that in School X these pretests and posttests have been carefully constructed and also administered with consummate care, but in School Y the teacher-made pretests and posttests have been carelessly tossed together and then administered in a slipshod fashion. In such a situation, we should surely weight the School X evidence of student growth more heavily than School Y's student-growth evidence.

As another illustration, the teacher-evaluation approach recently approved by the state of Washington allows local districts to choose among three different classroom-observation procedures for use in their teacher-evaluation programs. Well, suppose that one of those three observation techniques is far better supported by research evidence than the other two, and that this research-rooted classroom-observation procedure has been especially well installed and carried out in a given school district. Can you see that, in such a district, a teacher evaluator might be willing to assign more evaluative weight to the importance of results from these classroom observations than would be given to classroom-observation evidence from other districts?

And this, of course, is why a weighted-evidence approach to teacher evaluation is explicitly based on the *judgmental weighting* of evidence regarding a teacher's quality. The initial two steps in this teacher-appraisal strategy (shown in Figure 3.1) call, first, for the selection of the evaluative criterion/criteria to be employed and, second, for identification of evidence to represent a teacher's status regarding each evaluative criterion chosen. Step 3 of this process, then, involves determining the evidential weight, that is, the evaluative significance, we assign to each specific source of evidence based on a determination of what we regard as the worth of that evidence. Clearly, to arrive at sensible determinations of different evidence-sources' worthiness, we need to know what to look for when deciding on the strengths or weaknesses of particular kinds of evidence. And this is why, in the book's next five chapters, we'll be considering how to judge the persuasiveness of commonly employed sources of evidence regarding a teacher's quality.

Step 4: Deciding Whether to Make Adjustments in the Evaluative Weights of Evidence

Step 4 calls for a highly particularized judgment about the appropriate significance to assign to each evidence source when evaluating a particular teacher. The key question for a teacher evaluator to wrestle with at this point is whether to make any adjustments in the previously assigned weights (during Step 3) of the evidence that's now to be used. Not only does the quality of different evidence sources often vary from district to district, or from school to school, but the idiosyncratic nature of a teacher's instructional situation can frequently make a difference in the relative weight that should be assigned to specific evidence.

To illustrate, suppose that in a given high school the number of students who routinely enroll in nonrequired science courses has been consistently low. However, since the arrival three years ago of Miss Malone as a biology and physics teacher, the enrollment in her optional science courses has increased dramatically. Let's suppose, therefore, that the two evidence sources chosen by state (or district) teacher evaluators for use in the appraisal of this school's teachers have been "student absenteeism" and "student tardiness." What we see, when collecting this information about each teacher from official school documents, is that for Miss Malone's classes there has been an astonishing reduction in both absentee and tardiness data. Do you see, then, how it may be appropriate—for evaluating Miss Malone in this particular school—to weight attendance and tardiness data more heavily than might be the case for evaluating other teachers in that very same school—teachers in whose subjects the problems of absenteeism and tardiness have historically been less of a concern?

Please recognize that, in order to decide how much weight to give to competing sources of evidence, there may be occasions when a particular teacher's situation will warrant a decisively different relative weighting of evidence sources than was seen for other teachers in that same school or district. Yes, what is typically required in Step 4 is a decision about whether an *in-setting* adjustment of evidence weights should be used in the evaluation of a particular teacher. This necessity, when required, may appear to be too particularized to be objective, accurate, and fair. Yet, this is particularizing that's simply unavoidable. And this is why human beings are required when coping with the problem of how to most accurately mesh the significance of evaluative evidence with the particulars of a given teacher's instructional situation.

Step 5: Reaching a Coalesced Judgment of a Teacher's Quality

The final task in our five-step quest for evaluative accuracy calls for teacher evaluators to "put it all together" so that a final, overall evaluation of a teacher can be made—and can be made as accurately as possible. This wrap-up effort can be carried out at all levels of sophistication, but at its core the coalescing of diverse sorts of evidence, some of which carry more weight than others, is really quite straightforward. At a rudimentary level, teacher evaluators must assign evaluative weights (typically numerical allocations from a specified total-pool) to each evidence source being used, and also classify a teacher on each of those already weighted sources.

To illustrate, suppose teacher evaluators in a certain school district had selected one evaluative criterion, and five evidence sources to represent a teacher's status with respect to that criterion. Although each of the five sources had, early on, been given initial evaluative weights, an adjustment was made in the weighting for two of those sources because of the idiosyncratic nature of a teacher's instructional setting. To keep the classification of teachers on each evidence source simple, the following quality categories, and the points associated with them, were employed: Exceptionally Strong = 5 points, Strong = 4 points, Satisfactory = 3 points, Weak = 2 points, and Exceptionally Weak = 1 point.

In Figure 3.2 you will see a tabular representation of the evidence for a fictitious teacher, Maria Hill. Please note that the evaluative weights for all five evidence sources are presented in the form of percentages (in the second column from the left). These represent the number of potential points—out of 100—that could be earned by Maria for each evidence source. You will also see the evaluations of Maria's quality for each evidence source (from a high of 5 to a low of 1) have been given in the third column from the left. When the potential evaluative-weight points (40 points for state tests) are multiplied by the proportion of quality points earned (4/5 for state tests), the numerical contribution of each evidence source to Maria's total-point allocation is then available. (For instance, she earned 32 points for her students' scores on state tests.) As you can see,

Teacher: Maria Hill			Fourth Grade
Evidence Source	Evaluative Weight (times 100 points)	Teacher Quality (5 = High, 1 = Low)	Contribution to Overall Score
Classroom Observations	20%	4	20 x 4/5 = 16
Administrator Ratings*	20%	3	20 x 3/5 = 12
Student Ratings	10%	5	10 x 5/5 = 10
Student Growth			
• State Tests	40%	4	40 x 4/5 = 32
• Teacher-Made Tests**	10%	4	10 x 4/5 = 8
			Overall Score = 78 out of 100

*Original evidence weight lowered for this teacher
**Original evidence weight increased for this teacher

Figure 3.2   An Illustrative, Fictitious Evidence Summary for Maria Hill

because our fictitious Maria earned a satisfactory rating of 3 points from the administrator ratings evidence, she was awarded 12 of the 20 points obtainable, that is, 3/5 of the 20 possible points for that evidence source.

Maria's overall point allocation of 78 (out of 100), of course, will still need to be transformed into some sort of qualitative designation by teacher evaluators. And here, again, is where human judgment comes roaring into action. For the past several decades, American educators have been obliged to establish "performance standards" or "achievement levels" for the tests their students must take. In most of those standard-setting exercises, consideration is given to both standard-setters' hopes for students as well as to the realities of what constitutes a reasonable expectation regarding students' performances. In the case of teacher evaluation, no off-the-shelf performance levels will be found. Once more, drawing on lessons from the setting of students' performance levels, human judgment must be called on to signify what should constitute reasonable, varied levels of teachers' instructional ability.

As you can readily see, the judgmental challenges required when carrying out this kind of evaluation are considerable and, if not addressed appropriately, will usually lead to the inaccurate evaluation of a teacher. However, teacher evaluators need not regard the key operations of a weighted-evidence judgmental approach as too complicated, hence completely off-putting. When we strip this approach down to its absolute essentials, all that's involved is (1) deciding what's important when evaluating teachers, (2) choosing evidence to represent what's important, (3) weighing the significance of that evidence, (4) deciding whether any evidence weights need to be adjusted because of a teacher's distinctive instructional setting, and (5) combining different sorts of evidence to arrive at an overall evaluation of a teacher.

Those five steps can be gussied up considerably, and thus might be regarded by some as intimidating. Without such gussying, however, the five steps represent the way most of us actually evaluate anything that's really important to us. A weighted-evidence evaluation of teachers can be carried out elaborately with all sorts of flourishes, but it can also be applied in a simple, straightforward fashion.

In view of the importance of human judgment in implementing this approach to teacher evaluation, before adjourning this introductory description of weighted-evidence judgment, we need to give a bit of attention to the judges, that is, the teacher evaluators who take part in this sort of appraisal. Human judgment, of course, must be rendered by human beings. Accordingly, let's turn now to the important issue of "Who are the human beings who will be doing all this judging?"

WHO ARE THE JUDGES?

Because the teacher-evaluation strategy we're currently considering is awash with the need for human judgment, an obvious and important choice-point involves the designation of the human beings who will making the necessary judgments. And this is another key choice-point in a weighted-evidence judgmental approach to teacher evaluation. Putting it as simply as possible, when carrying out this teacher-appraisal strategy, you do what you can afford to do. The more judges you have, the better will be your evaluations. The better prepared and better monitored those judges are, the better will be your evaluations. In short, fully recognizing the potential hassles and costs associated with teacher evaluation, the more resources that can be invested in the selection and preparation of those rendering the required judgments, the better will be the resultant evaluations.

In most of today's recently created teacher-evaluation systems, few states have the luxury of coming up with a lavish evaluative operation. More often or not, therefore, these systems will need to get by using minimal dollars. Even so, a judgmentally based appraisal system offers the best hope of evaluating teachers as accurately as possible and in a manner that helps rather than harms the quality of instruction offered by a state's schools.

At the most basic level, a school-site administrator, working totally alone, could adhere as closely as possible to the five-step approach described in this chapter. Would it be difficult for a principal or assistant principal to do this evaluative job all alone? Of course it would. But if this is the only way that weighted-evidence judgment can be carried out, it will still lead to more accurate evaluations of teachers than will other strategies not as attuned to the differential quality of evidence and the possible need to weight such evidence in a particular teacher's instructional setting.

If resources permit, it would be far better to establish review panels composed of experienced educators, that is, teachers or administrators, who would be trained and (if resources permit) certificated to carry out the necessary judgmental determinations. Ideally, the decisions rendered by these review panels (perhaps composed of 3–6 members) could be periodically monitored by an independent group charged with verifying that a review panel's members had been appropriately attentive to the available evidence as they arrived at their judgments.

The essence of weighted-evidence judgmental teacher evaluation is to allow experienced educators, trained as well as possible, to provide thoughtful evidence-informed judgments regarding the caliber of a specific teacher operating in that teacher's distinctive instructional setting. The better that these judgments are made, the better will be the ensuing teacher evaluations.

It would be understandable, however, if some skeptics might dismiss "teachers-evaluating-teachers" as an insufficiently objective enterprise. The incredulity of those skeptics, of course, typically comes from a concern that many teachers would be disinclined to render negative judgments about their fellow teachers—even about teachers from different schools. Nevertheless, genuine objectivity and optimal accuracy will be needed for the evaluation of public school teachers whose salaries are paid for with citizens' tax dollars. Accordingly, to the degree possible, check-points should be installed in any weighted-evidence judgmental approach to teacher evaluation so that sufficient objectivity-assurance information can be made available to interested parties.

Human judgment is at the heart of the teacher-evaluation strategy that's being advocated here, and care must be exercised so that the judgments made are as accurate as they can be, and demonstrably free of self-service. Thus, inclusion at key points of noneducator citizens, for instance, parents and members of the local business community, can markedly enhance the credibility of the ongoing evaluations. Not only must evidence-weighted judgmental teacher evaluations be as objective and as accurate as possible, they must be *seen* to be as objective and as accurate as possible.

CHAPTER IMPLICATIONS FOR THREE AUDIENCES

For Policymakers: Because this chapter describes the fundamental nature of a teacher-evaluation system unabashedly rooted in human judgment, educational policymakers need to start deciding whether they believe an evaluative system akin to weighted-evidence judgment has sufficient merit. Putting it differently, policymakers need to begin arriving at their own judgments about whether the five-step evaluation strategy set forth in the chapter is suitable for widespread use. If weighted-evidence judgment is regarded positively, then policymakers need to be watchful regarding whether a particular incarnation of such an approach—at a state level—is carried out suitably. Because evidence is so important in a weighted-evidence approach to teacher evaluation, policymakers should pay particular attention to the quality of evidence being employed in the teacher-evaluation system in which they are most interested.

For Administrators: In many, if not most, instances, teacher evaluations will be carried out by school-site administrators—often guided by district-level administrators who are taking their cues from a state's official teacher-evaluation framework. What this means, of course, is that the heavy evaluative lifting is likely to be done by schools' principals and assistant principals. If any variant of a weighted-evidence judgmental approach is to be employed in a district or school, then local educational administrators should become completely conversant with the five-step operation set forth in Figure 3.1. Because this set of operations should function as a local evaluator's action guide, its mastery is clearly important. If, however, having read this chapter and considered the virtues of weighted-evidence judgmental evaluation, an administrator rejects this evaluative strategy, then such an administrator needs to explore the viability of alternative evaluative approaches—those that are compatible with a state-sanctioned approach.

For Teachers: Conceding that, for most of us, it is far from fun to be evaluated, teachers might wish to consider what alternatives to weighted-evidence judgment they would regard as an acceptable teacher-evaluation strategy. Although human judgments can particularize evaluations so that they more sensitively take into consideration a given teacher's distinctive situation, the same judgmental strategy can clearly lead to erroneous judgments. Clearly, any evaluation system that is based heavily on the judgments rendered by human beings is likely to be less than perfect. But this suggests that teachers need to become sufficiently well versed in the viscera of whatever evaluation system is being used so that if, in their view, evaluative judgments have been mistaken, appropriate appeal procedures can be invoked to rectify as many mistakes as possible.

CHAPTER 4

Evidence From Standardized Tests

In this chapter, and the four chapters following it, you'll be taking a look at different kinds of evidence that might be used when evaluating teachers. In each of these five chapters, a description of the essential features of the evidence that's treated in the chapter will be followed by a set of *Guidelines for Evidential Weighting*. These guidelines will suggest when to give increased evaluative weight to certain variations of the evidence being treated in the chapter. The teacher-evaluation model being endorsed in this book, as you know, often calls for teacher evaluators to make numerous judgments regarding how much evaluative influence should be assigned to specific sorts of evidence. Accordingly, it is important for those concerned with the evaluation of teachers to become reasonably conversant with the major strengths and weaknesses of the evidence that's potentially indicative of a teacher's quality. In the five chapters dealing with evaluative evidence, the following sources of evidence will be considered in turn: standardized tests, classroom assessments, classroom observations, ratings, and other evidence sources.

After completing these five chapters, you will most likely have formed your own opinions about the evidence sources that, in your opinion, are apt to provide the most persuasive evidence regarding a teacher's effectiveness. Remember, before choosing among potential evidence sources, a teacher evaluator must first identify the evaluative criterion (or the evaluative criteria) on which to base the evaluation. The selection of suitable evidence sources must obviously coincide with the specific evaluative criteria adopted as the basis for an evaluation.

Because the approach to teacher evaluation being recommended in this book calls for weighted-evidence judgment based on a single evaluative criterion, namely, *instructional ability,* the suitability of the evidence in these five evidence-focused chapters will assume that this criterion has already been selected as the focus for a teacher-evaluation program. If two or more evaluative criteria had been adopted, then the evidence-selection activities employed to select and weight evidence sources for a single evaluative criterion (in this instance, the criterion of *instructional ability*) would need to be repeated for any evaluative criteria chosen.

In Figure 4.1 you can see a graphic representation of how five potential evidence sources might help determine a teacher's instructional ability. Each of the five potential sources of evidence, in turn, should be considered by teacher evaluators, and then included or excluded from a planned teacher-evaluation procedure.

But whether a teacher-evaluation process is to be based on only one evaluative criterion, or on several evaluative criteria, an important preliminary step is to *clarify the nature of the evaluative criteria being used in the evaluation.* This seemingly obvious clarification activity is, regrettably, often overlooked. Such an omission usually occurs because too many participants in a teacher evaluation blithely assume that what's in their own heads regarding the meaning of a particular evaluative criterion accurately coincides with what other people believe regarding that evaluative criterion. Even properly conceived teacher evaluation can stumble getting out of the gate

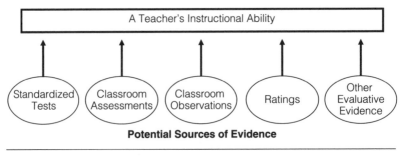

Figure 4.1   Potential Evidence Sources for the Evaluative Criterion of a Teacher's Instructional Ability

simply because those designing and operating the evaluation have discordant conceptions about what's meant by a key evaluative criterion.

With this brief introduction to the five-chapter suite focused on possible evidence sources, it is time to turn to this chapter's very own evidence source, namely, *students' performances on standardized tests*. As will be true with the other four evidence-source chapters, we will begin with a general description of the chief attributes of the chapter's evidence source, then consider the relevance of such evidence to the evaluative criterion selected, namely, a teacher's *instructional ability*.

KEY TESTING TENETS

One of the most serious impediments when dealing with a topic that's familiar to most people, whether it's coping with the weather, shopping in grocery stores, or going to the movies, is that such familiarity can often lead to serious misunderstandings. Indeed, from the perspective of someone who's trying to explain something, it's usually better if the recipient of the explanation knows naught about what's being explained. Partial knowledge, unfortunately, often corrupts comprehension. And so it is with the topic of "educational testing." Most people think they know a fair amount about educational testing. But whether it's called educational testing, educational assessment, or educational measurement (all of which are essentially synonymous labels), the truth is that most people know far less about this topic than they think they do.

Because most of today's adults have, earlier in their lives, personally completed school-administered tests for about a dozen or more years, many of those adults think they understand educational testing pretty well. More often than not, their assumed levels of understanding are unwarranted.

Thus, without discounting your personal understanding of what goes on when we give educational tests to students, let me ask you a favor. Just for a few pages, will you please blot out what you already know about educational tests? Seriously, please put your preconceptions about educational assessment on hold for a few pages. You'll be more likely to appreciate the sometimes subtle, yet significant distinctions that are about to be made.

Why We Test

Educators test students in order to make inferences about students' *covert* status based on students' *overt* responses to tests. Because teachers typically attempt to promote their students' (1) increased knowledge, (2) acquisition of significant skills, and (3) development of appropriate attitudes, teachers often need to get a fix on students' knowledge, skills, and attitudes. This permits a teacher's next-step instructional decisions to mesh well with students' current status. For example, why teach students something they already know? Teachers, obviously, can't make good instructional decisions if they don't know certain things about their students' current status.

But, unfortunately, we can't determine what a student knows or can do merely by looking at a student—even looking carefully. This is because almost all of the really important outcomes educators seek for their students are covert, that is, are unable to be seen. Teachers can't look at a third grader and then determine whether this child can read with comprehension. So, rather than guessing about the reading ability of a given student, we typically give that child a reading test that asks the child to read a passage, for instance, a short story, and then respond to a series of questions about the passage. It is the child's overt responses to the test's questions that allow us to arrive at an inference about the child's covert reading skill. Using such test-based inferences about students' unseen reading abilities, teachers can then introduce instructional activities that best fit their students' current knowledge, skills, and attitudes. And this is why teachers test students—because the results of those tests help teachers come up with more appropriate instruction for their students.

One of the most important requisites of a test to be used in the evaluation of a state's teachers is that the test be *aligned* with the state's approved curricular targets (or content standards), that is, the test's items represent the official knowledge and skills the state's students are supposed to learn while in school. Most important tests these days, particularly those that are to be used in evaluating the success of schools or, now, teachers, are accompanied by evidence showing that they do, indeed, measure students' mastery of a state's official curricular aims.

For educational tests to supply inferences about test takers, over the years the individuals involved in educational testing have developed a collection of technical procedures described as *psychometrics*. Indeed, most of today's psychometric thinking about educational measurement in the United States can be traced back almost a full century. Much of this traditional psychometric thinking is enormously useful. However, when evaluating teachers, as you will soon see, traditional psychometrics can sometimes get in the way.

A Psychometric Blessed Trinity

The three time-honored psychometric concepts on which today's educational tests have traditionally been developed are *reliability, validity,* and *absence of bias.* Reliability refers to the degree to which a test measures with *consistency* whatever it happens to be measuring. Validity represents the *accuracy* with which a test-based inference is made about students. Finally, absence of bias allows us to tell whether a test is *fair* to certain groups of students based on such personal attributes as race, gender, or religion.

Reliability, validity, and absence of bias constitute the most fundamental concepts of educational testing and, as such, represent a test's technical adequacy. Each of these three attributes, however, can be calculated in fundamentally different ways, and it really is unrealistic for me to try to jam an educational assessment short-course into a few paragraphs. Accordingly, for those readers who wish to verify the suitability of any standardized test's technical adequacy, two likely courses of action are at hand. First, an assessment consultant could be enlisted to verify that a standardized test passes muster with respect to reliability, validity, and absence of bias. Numerous such consultants can be located in most parts of the nation. Second, if someone wishes to personally analyze a test's technical adequacy, the knowledge necessary to do so can be acquired from assessment textbooks or by completing a course in educational assessment. Putting it differently, to appraise a standardized test's technical qualities, one either can personally become assessment literate or can secure the assistance of someone who possesses assessment expertise.

STANDARDIZED TESTS—TWO TRIBES, TWO TASKS

Although the ESEA Flexibility Program's recommendations regarding teacher-evaluation strategies do *not* say flatly that the evidence of student growth in a state's teacher-evaluation process *must* include students' scores on standardized tests, most educators seem to think those federal guidelines do, indeed, call for this sort of evidence. Such an interpretation of federal preferences is altogether under-standable in view of the greater credibility generally attributed to students' standardized-test scores rather than to students' scores on teacher-built classroom tests.

Moreover, because NCLB requires that states must administer annual accountability tests, at least in reading and mathematics, in grades 3–8 and once in high school, such accountability testing has been up and running in all states for more than a decade. The ready availability of students' scores on those NCLB-mandated accountability tests has given such tests front-and-center attention from planners of many states' teacher-appraisal procedures. Thus, if a state's annual accountability tests are administered in the spring, which most of them are, then a measure of students' year-to-year growth can readily be calculated for all teachers whose students are obliged to take those annual tests. (Students' scores on this year's accountability tests are simply contrasted with those same students' scores on last year's accountability tests.) So, although use of a state's annually administered accountability tests need not constitute the exclusive student-growth evidence for all teachers (many of those teachers, of course, teach students or subjects not assessed by NCLB tests), the use of standardized accountability tests will clearly go a long way in supplying the needed student-growth data for many teachers. In the next chapter we'll consider how to obtain student-growth evidence for teachers in "non-tested grades and subjects," that is, teachers whose students are not obliged to complete a state's annual NCLB tests.

What, precisely, is a "standardized test"? Put simply, it's a test that's administered, scored, and interpreted in a regular, prede-termined manner. Two kinds of standardized tests are used most frequently by educators, namely, standardized *aptitude tests* and standardized *achievement tests*. These two tests have very different assessment functions. The measurement mission of a standardized aptitude test is to allow predictions to be made about test-takers' future performances. For example, the SAT and ACT are college admission examinations that, when given to high school students, predict how successful those students will be when they get to col-lege. Aptitude tests, therefore, are patently designed to be *predictive* by measuring whether a test-taker has the aptitude for subsequent success. Standardized achievement tests, in contrast, are intended to help us identify what students know and can do, that is, such tests assess students' *current knowledge and skills*. In a sense, then, standardized achievement tests are intended to allow us to make score-based inferences regarding a test-taker's current knowledge and skills, while standardized aptitude tests permit inferences forecasting a test-taker's future performance—often in a subsequent academic setting.

Standardized tests come to us from two sources. First, commercial testing companies such as CTB/McGraw-Hill create and then sell a number of off-the-shelf standardized tests to states or school districts. Such assessment firms usually sell both standardized aptitude tests and standardized achievement tests. In some instances, these companies provide nationwide, officially administered testing opportunities so that, for instance, high school students all across the country can complete the SAT or ACT (as well as versions of those two tests designed for younger students). A second source of standardized tests, particularly standardized achievement tests, are state departments of education who usually contract with one of the nation's assessment companies to construct state-customized standardized tests for their particular state.

Sometimes a state's NCLB tests will be standardized achievement tests that, built from scratch, are intended to yield inferences about students' mastery of a state's official curricular aims, that is, its state-approved content standards. In other instances, a state's NCLB accountability tests will be slightly augmented versions of off-the-shelf nationally standardized achievement tests. A handful of new items are usually added to such national tests in an attempt to make the tests better match a state's official content standards. For example, the nationally available *Iowa Tests of Basic Skills* might be chosen as a given state's NCLB accountability tests, but minor item-additions in the commercially available versions of those tests will be made to better reflect a state's distinctive curricular preferences.

It might be reasonably assumed that, in order to satisfy NCLB's requirements for each state to evaluate its students' mastery of that state's content standards, those NCLB assessments would typically be *achievement* tests rather than *aptitude* tests. And, in general, this assumption turns out to be well grounded. Most NCLB accountability tests, whether created internally by state personnel or purchased from external assessment vendors, will be achievement tests. Interestingly, however, if a state's educational officials believe that what's measured by a standard-ized *aptitude* test represents a state's content standards, then even aptitude tests can be used as NCLB accountability tests. Some states, for instance, are using the ACT tests to help satisfy their NCLB assessment requirements.

Finally, relying chiefly on federal funds, two state-directed assessment consortia are currently creating assessments (scheduled for availability in the 2014–15 school year) intended to measure students' mastery of the Common Core State Standards that have been accepted as curricular aims by all but a handful of our 50 states. If these consortium-built tests are available on schedule, then they will represent another potent assessment alternative for measuring students' growth. The two sets of assessments currently being gener-ated by these two well funded multi-state assessment consortia are clearly intended to be achievement tests rather than aptitude tests. So, during the 2014–15 school year, states' teacher-evaluation pro-grams attempting to represent students' growth via their scores on standardized achievement tests will have another significant assess-ment choice at their disposal because of the availability of these consortium-built tests.

Summing up, then, to the degree that the architects of a teacher-evaluation process wish to include students' growth as a significant factor in the evaluation of a given teacher, then reliance on students' scores on standardized tests to supply the evidence of students' growth will surely be a prominent option. Therein, however, resides a subtle trap for those who would evaluate teachers. And this trap, simply put, is that if the standardized tests selected for this use are not up to the task of evaluating teachers, then those tests should have *no* role in determining a teacher's quality. Let's see why.

TRADITIONAL TEST BUILDING AND ITS OFF-TASK ALLURE

Several pages earlier, you were encouraged to do a bit of blocking out when it came to what you know about educational testing. Now you're going to see why such a suspension of knowledge can be helpful. You're going to learn about the essential mission of educa-tional measurement that's been dominant in America for about 100 years. It is a mission, unfortunately, that does not coincide with the kinds of tests needed to evaluate teachers.

The Origins of Traditional Educational Testing

Let's head back in time, for almost a full century, and you'll discover a pivotal test that has enormously influenced our thinking about educational testing. This high-impact test was administered during World War I (not WWII, but WWI). It was the *Army Alpha,* and it was developed during WWI to help U.S. Army leaders identify the most suitable candidates for the Army's officer training programs. Our nation had, at that time, become engaged in an unprecedented worldwide conflict and, therefore, faced a need to place huge numbers of men in the military. Army officials were stumped, however, about how to identify the recruits who would most effectively be trained as the junior officers who would lead U.S. troops in battle. Faced with this problem, Army leaders sought help from the American Psychological Association, which appointed a test-development committee that, during roughly a week of work at the Vineland Training School in Vineland, New Jersey, created the *Army Alpha.* The *Alpha* was a group-administrable, objectively scored mental *aptitude* test that presented a series of verbal and quantitative tasks to recruits so that a determination could be made about those test-takers' likelihood of success in the Army's officer training programs. For example, when compared with other test takers, a recruit whose *Alpha* score was very high, let's say at the 96th percentile, would be regarded as a far better candidate for officer training than would a recruit whose *Alpha* score was lower at, say, the 43rd percentile. The purpose of the *Army Alpha,* then, was to provide inferences about test-takers' scores relative to the scores of other test takers, that is, this ground-breaking standardized test was designed to supply *comparative score interpretations.*

The *Alpha* was administered to about 1,750,000 men during WWI, and it worked remarkably well. It was so successful, indeed, that this *aptitude* test's comparative-interpretation strategy was adopted a few years later by those who created educational *achievement* tests. For instance, the very first version of the *Stanford Achievement Tests,* a widely used and frequently updated set of nationally standardized achievement tests, was published in 1923, only a few years after the close of WWI. The assessment strategy employed in educational aptitude tests (such as the numerous "intelligence tests" published in subsequent years by many testing organizations) as well as educational achievement tests (such as the nationally standardized achievement tests soon to emerge from many test publishers) was unabashedly aimed at providing comparative score interpretations. A quest for such interpretations soon became the governing goal of traditional educational testing—and it still is.

That's right, the way today's educational tests are initially created, and then revised until they work satisfactorily, is almost exclusively focused on providing test users with comparative score-based interpretations. This is not the time or place to lay out the many moments in the creation and refinement of standardized tests—whether they're aptitude tests or achievement tests—that the pursuit of comparative score interpretations leads to decisions that render those tests less useful for purposes of teacher evaluation. The following illustration, however, may help make this point.

Dealing With Effective Instruction

In order for a test to yield scores from which comparative score interpretations can be made most efficiently (so we can test students for only 50 or so minutes rather than for three or four hours), test-takers' responses to each item on the test should yield a considerable amount of variation. That is, if a test is going to do a good job in permitting a test's users to make accurate comparative score interpretations, the test needs to yield *total-test* scores in which there is a considerable degree of *score spread,* that is, so there are numerous high scores, numerous low scores, and numerous middling scores. For purposes of comparative score interpretations, we don't want too many students to answer a particular item incorrectly or, conversely, we don't want too many students to answer a particular item correctly.

To illustrate, let's assume that students' mastery of an important cognitive skill has been chosen to be measured on a state-customized standardized achievement test, and that two items (Number 17 and Number 32) have been included on the test to help assess students' mastery of this significant cognitive skill. Generally speaking, most students don't respond correctly to those two items. Well, if the cognitive skill is truly so very significant, we might see state-level instructional specialists providing a new program to help the state's teachers promote students' mastery of this important cognitive skill. Moreover, if the state's new program is really effective, then after a few years we are likely to see exceptionally high percentages of the state's students now *correctly* answering those two items measuring students' mastery of this cognitive skill. Given these circumstances, that is, a state-led instructional intervention that's getting more students to master an important cognitive skill, when the test is updated, what do you think will happen to the two items on which the state's students are now scoring so well?

Sadly, odds are that if such dramatically increased proportions of the state's students are currently scoring well on Items 17 and 32—because huge numbers of those students will now have mastered the skill being measured by those items—then the two items will almost certainly be jettisoned when the test is updated. That's right, because too many students are now answering Items 17 and 32 correctly, those items will no longer be making their original contributions to spreading out test-takers' performances on the total test. Traditional psychometrics, and its preoccupation with providing comparative score interpretations, will have won the day. Test items that did an accurate job of measuring teachers' skill in promoting students' mastery of a key skill will have been discarded.

Ensuring Score Spread From the Get-Go

Because the pursuit of score spread is so central to traditional educational testing—whether aptitude-testing or achievement-testing—those who create standardized tests often try to build in items from the earliest test-development stages that are likely to make contributions to test-takers' score spread on the total test. Incidentally, when describing how well test takers perform on each of a test's items, historically we do so by using an item's p value, that is, the percentage of test takers who answer the item correctly. (An item that had a p value of .75, for example, would have been answered correctly by 75% of the students answering that item.) In order to increase the probability of getting suitable score spread from the students who take a standardized test, test developers often try to create items that will end up with p values in the .40–.60 range rather than items with very high or very low p values.

Besides having most of a standardized test's items represent the middle-difficulty range, two additional ways of getting an adequate score spread from a standardized test are often employed. But these two tactics turn out to be frequently misleading when, as part of a teacher appraisal, we use standardized tests to ascertain student growth. Let's look briefly at each of these tactics whereby those who construct standardized tests can attain the score spread for which they yearn—yet at the same time produce test results apt to *distort* the evaluation of teachers. Two kinds of items that, almost certainly, will contribute to score spread on a standardized test are (1) items linked to students' socioeconomic status—their SES—and (2) items linked to students' inherited academic aptitudes. A brief description of each of these item types, along with an example of each, will illustrate this problem.

SES-linked items. Socioeconomic status (SES), with few exceptions, is a nicely spread-out variable—a variable that doesn't change all that often or very substantially. Students who come from high-SES families will, in general, have access to experiences and content more likely to be addressed in educational test items than will students who come from lower-SES families. Consider, for instance, the item in Figure 4.2, which is a slightly massaged version of an actual item appearing on one of the nation's standardized fourth-grade tests in reading.

Can you see that the vocabulary item in Figure 4.2 is intended to assess a fourth grader's knowledge of the word "field" when the word is used in a vocational context? Verifying the size of a student's vocabulary with items such as this is a common technique in standardized achievement tests. But let's recognize that fourth graders from more affluent families are likely to have one or more parents working successfully in such "fields" as law, teaching, and journalism. If your mom or dad is an accountant, a doctor, or a lawyer, they'll often refer in family conversations to their "field" of employment.

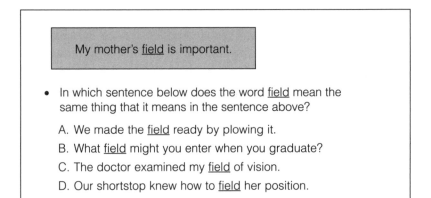

> My mother's field is important.

- In which sentence below does the word field mean the same thing that it means in the sentence above?

  A. We made the field ready by plowing it.

  B. What field might you enter when you graduate?

  C. The doctor examined my field of vision.

  D. Our shortstop knew how to field her position.

Figure 4.2   An SES-Linked Item From a Standardized Fourth-Grade Reading Test

However, please take a quick mental trip to the other end of the SES ladder, that is, to a less affluent family in which the father works in a car-wash and the mother works as a cashier in a grocery store. Those parents do not have "fields"; they have *jobs*. You can safely bet that in the lower SES family, there'll rarely be a reference to someone's "field" of employment.

As a consequence, students from higher SES backgrounds will be more likely to answer Figure 4.2's item correctly than will their lower SES counterparts—not because the more affluent students were taught better, but simply because they were more likely at home to bump into this particular item's usage of the word "field."

Although it is true that the developers of standardized tests may not deliberately set out to generate SES-linked items, be assured that items such as these sometimes end up being used on standardized tests because, in recognition that SES is such a nicely spread-out variable, such items are almost certain to contribute to a test's over-all score spread. These items may indicate little or nothing about a teacher's instructional ability, but they do contribute to a test's ability to provide comparative score interpretations. Remember, the vast majority of educational assessment specialists are striving to do one thing, and one thing alone: create tests that provide comparative score interpretations.

Aptitude-linked items. Another kind of item that's apt to be a big contributor to a standardized test's overall score spread is an item that's linked to students' *inherited academic aptitudes.* Let's face it; some kids are luckier in the gene-pool sweepstakes than are other kids. Because there is a considerable spread, from birth, of students' *inherited* academic aptitudes such as their innate verbal, quantitative, or spatial aptitudes, then items linked to one or more of those apti-tudes will contribute to the sort of total score spread being sought by the developers of standardized tests. Let's look at Figure 4.3 contain-ing a fourth-grade item, mildly altered, from a nationally standard-ized achievement test for fourth-grade mathematics.

As you can see, answering this item correctly will be much easier for students who were *born* with a hefty hunk of spatial-visualization aptitude. Fourth-graders who, from birth, are able to spatially visual-ize such objects as those required for this mental letter-folding task will tend to do far better in realizing that the upper-case B (found in answer-choice C) will, when folded, have two halves that are perfectly matched. In contrast, fourth-graders whose innate spatial-visualization aptitudes are less strong will have more difficulty in determining the consequences of mentally folding the B.

Just as we saw in the case of SES-linked items, a test's items correlated with students' in-born verbal, quantitative, or spatial aptitudes will typically lead to the sort of total-test spread in scores needed for a test to provide the comparative score interpretations that, for almost a full century, have dominated education testing. Because inherited academic aptitudes are spread out significantly from the moment of a child's birth, then test items linked to such academic aptitudes are almost certain to help spread out students' total scores on standardized tests. But those items will not help us evaluate a teacher's instructional ability.

In review, you can see that when traditional psychometricians construct standardized tests—either aptitude or achievement tests—the overarching mission of providing comparative score interpretations can, over time, lead to the inclusion on such tests of items linked to students' inherited academic aptitudes and to students' SES. Although such items, because of the substantial variability present in SES and inherited aptitudes, will contribute to the score spread of students' total-test scores, both of those variables represent

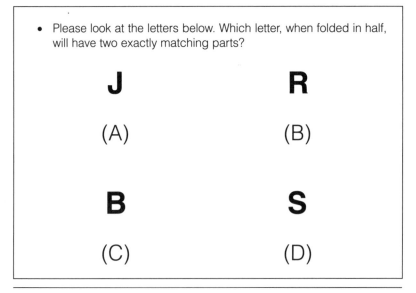

- Please look at the letters below. Which letter, when folded in half, will have two exactly matching parts?

J
(A)

R
(B)

B
(C)

S
(D)

Figure 4.3   An Aptitude-Linked Item From a Nationally Standardized Fourth-Grade Mathematics Test

what students bring to school, rather than what students learn once they arrive at school. If the evaluation of teachers has been centered on determining a teacher's instructional ability, a standardized test that measures students' entry status—rather than measuring what students have learned in school—is actually apt to supply misleading evidence about a teacher's effectiveness.

Instructional Sensitivity as a Requisite

Before leaving our consideration of standardized tests as a source of evidence for the evaluation of teachers, we need to identify an important attribute of such tests that should be regarded as truly *essential* when appraising teachers. What is this attribute that's so significant when we decide to use students' standardized test scores to help evaluate teachers? The attribute is a standardized test's *instructional sensitivity*. And here's what it is:

Instructional sensitivity is the degree to which students' performances on a test accurately reflect the quality of instruction specifically provided to promote students' mastery of what is being assessed.

Put plainly, instructional sensitivity indicates the ability of a test to distinguish between well-taught and badly taught students. If a standardized test is instructionally *sensitive,* that is, if it can help us differentiate students who were effectively taught from students who were ineffectively taught, then this test can make a contribution to the appraisal of a teacher's instructional ability. If a standardized test is instructionally *insensitive,* however, it should have no role at all—none whatsoever—in evaluating the instructional ability of a teacher.

Instructional sensitivity is not an on/off variable. Tests are not totally instructionally sensitive or totally instructionally insensitive. Rather, standardized tests can vary in the degree to which they are instructionally sensitive. For example, if you were considering a standardized test for possible inclusion in a teacher-evaluation program, and a careful analysis of the test indicated it contained many items that were SES linked and aptitude linked, odds are that this test would be less instructionally sensitive than would a test containing fewer of those items.

How, then, is evidence of a standardized test's instructional sensitivity assembled? Well, first we can employ a *judgmental* evidence-gathering technique in which we assemble review teams of experienced teachers who judge, item-by-item, whether well-taught students ought to be able to answer an item correctly. Second, we use an *empirical* evidence-collection procedure in which we initially identify two extreme groups of teachers whose students, over a period of several years, have (or haven't) shown marked test-score improvements. Thus, for purposes of this analysis, we have isolated two groups of particularly strong and particularly weak teachers. We then employ statistical analyses to discern which field-tested items are *not* answered correctly more often by students of the stronger teachers than by students of the weaker teachers. During such a field test, apparently instructionally insensitive items are then removed from the pool of test-eligible items. (A colleague and I have described elsewhere how such analyses can be used to collect evidence of items' instructional sensitivity; see Popham & Ryan, 2012.)

Standardized tests not *demonstrably* instructionally sensitive are as likely to provide incorrect inferences about a teacher's quality as they are to provide correct inferences about a teacher's quality. And this is why, in a nutshell, when a standardized test is being considered to collect significant evidence of students' growth in a properly conceived teacher-evaluation system, evidence of sufficient instructional sensitivity must be regarded as absolutely requisite.

RETURNING TO VALIDITY

Well, you've now completed this chapter's race through the highlights of educational testing and why it is, at bottom, educational testing must lead to test-takers' scores from which valid inferences about those test takers can be gleaned. Tests for which insufficient evidence of validity is available should never be used for making important decisions. And evaluating the caliber of a teacher is an unquestionably important decision.

And here's where traditional psychometrics raises its *Army Alpha* head once more. We definitely need tests that can provide us with accurate comparative score distinctions. Such tests come in handy whenever we deal with situations in which we have more applicants than openings. For instance, traditional score-sorting tests are useful when we must choose among too many applicants who want to get into medical school or who wish to become members of "elite special forces" in the military. But merely because a test can help sort out applicants for limited-opening settings does not mean the test can tell us how effective a teacher is.

Even if a standardized test (whether state customized or nationally standardized) is accompanied by evidence that it is "aligned" to a state's official curricular aims, this does *not* signify that the test does, in fact, discriminate between effectively taught and ineffectively taught students. Clearly, if a state's teachers are organizing their instruction to promote students' mastery of a state's content standards, then it is likely a content-aligned standardized test will be more instructionally sensitive than will be a test unaligned to those content standards. Nonetheless, content alignment is only a necessary, not a sufficient condition to satisfy the usage of a standardized test for the evaluation of teachers.

In sum, the traditional measurement mission of educational tests, though not without its applications, is not consonant with the evaluation of teachers' instructional ability. Only those standardized tests for which there is sufficient validity evidence, and in this instance such evidence revolves around a test's demonstrable instructional sensitivity, should be used to evaluate teachers. Absent such evidence, standardized tests should have no role in the evaluation of America's teachers.

EVIDENTIAL-WEIGHT GUIDELINES

When considering whether to incorporate students' scores from this chapter's evidence source (standardized tests) as an indication of a teacher's instructional ability and, if having decided to do so, how much evaluative influence to assign to this evidence, the following guidelines are offered. The evaluative influence to be recommended will be referred to as *evidential weight* and will assume that, based on an overall consideration of the evaluative yield of the evidence source under consideration, it has been decided to include this evidence source in the evaluation of teachers.

- Greater evidential weight should be given to students' standardized-test scores for which alignment evidence indicates a test's items accurately represent students' mastery of a state's curricular aims.

- Greater evidential weight should be given to students' scores on standardized tests if evidence demonstrates that those tests satisfy traditional psychometric technical expectations associated with reliability, validity, and absence of bias.
- Greater evidential weight should be given to students' performances on standardized tests when validity evidence indicates that the tests are instructionally sensitive.

CHAPTER IMPLICATIONS FOR THREE AUDIENCES

For Policymakers: Because evidence about teachers' effectiveness based on students' standardized-test scores frequently generates positive images of accuracy and objectivity, many educational policymakers view scores on such tests as the most important kind of teacher-evaluation evidence. Yet, as this chapter points out, only when a standardized test (1) is aligned to a state's content standards, (2) satisfies technical (psychometric) requirements, and (3) has been shown to be instructional sensitive should that test play a prominent role in evaluating teachers. Clearly, when a test is labeled as "an achievement test," policymakers will often conclude that the "achievement" the test measures was acquired by students because of instruction that took place in school. Yet, to the extent that a standardized test measures what students bring to school rather than what they were taught there, such tests should contribute little to the evaluation of teachers. Educational policymakers must understand the key ideas in this chapter so that they can use such knowledge not only in shaping their own policy stances but also in influencing the policy positions of others.

For Administrators: To the degree that educational administrators, either in the district office or in the schools, will have a hand in implementing a state's teacher-evaluation procedures, it will benefit those administrators to have a solid grasp on the key evidence being used in such evaluations. Thus, because of the near certainty that administrators will be involved in carrying out the teacher-evaluation enterprise, those administrators should surely become conversant with the key attributes of standardized tests because students' scores on such tests will often be advocated—sometimes unthinkingly—as the pivotal evidence for evaluating teachers. So, for example, if it is learned that a state's annual accountability tests are accompanied by no evidence supporting their instructional sensitivity, this would give administrators an ideal opportunity to try to persuade a state's educational officials that students' scores on such tests should have only a modest influence on a teacher's evaluation. As a consequence, educational administrators should not only urge that other evidence-gathering methods should be given greater evaluative weight, but should attempt to improve the quality of evidence supplied by those alternate evidence-production procedures.

For Teachers: Teachers who are not particularly familiar with the basic concepts and procedures of educational assessment should most definitely become so. Although recently trained teachers are beginning to receive rudimentary knowledge about educational measurement, today's emphasis on teacher evaluation, and especially on *test-based* teacher evaluation, means that most of the nation's teachers will soon be judged—whether they like it or not—at least in part according to their students' test scores. This chapter, because it treats the particular kind of evaluative evidence likely to be featured in most states' teacher-appraisal systems, shows teachers how imperative it is that they not allow themselves to be unknowledgeable about educational assessment. An assessment-literate teacher can explain to others—administrators and parents—why it is that students' performances on certain types of standardized tests should have little or no role in teacher evaluations. An assessment-illiterate teacher can't. Given the certainty that student growth will continue to be a pivotal component of most states' teacher-appraisal schemes, and the certainty that students' test performances will be the chief indicator by which student growth is determined, teachers simply must become more knowledgeable about the basics of educational assessment. Those basics are neither intimidating nor numerically mind-numbing. Teachers need to understand more about educational assessment.

CHAPTER 5

Evidence From Classroom Assessments

In this chapter, as in the previous chapter, we will be considering a potential source of evidence that might be employed when determining a teacher's quality. And, because students' learning is so patently important when evaluating a teacher's competence, we will once again be looking at ways of measuring what students have learned. Even if there were no federal urging—as there currently is—that students' growth should be a significant factor in states' teacher-evaluation programs, teacher evaluators who overlook students' learning when appraising teachers would be dim-witted. Students' learning, typically evidenced by improvements in students' test scores, should play a powerful role when any teacher is evaluated.

In Chapter 4 we were looking at evidence of students' growth when collected by the use of standardized assessments such as states' annual accountability tests. In this chapter we will deal with the collection of student-growth evidence through the use of *classroom assessments*. Both standardized assessments and classroom assessments, if appropriately developed and appropriately used, can supply compelling evidence regarding a teacher's quality.

STAKING OUT THE NATURE OF "CLASSROOM ASSESSMENT"

A major distinction between standardized tests and classroom assessments hinges on the regularization that one group of tests possesses and the other group of tests doesn't. Standardized tests are administered, scored, and interpreted in a standard, predetermined manner. Such standardization is not necessary when using classroom assessments.

It is sometimes thought that all classroom assessments must be built solo by a teacher who, without assistance from others, works independently at home or in a corner of the school's teachers' lounge. This is not how we will be viewing classroom assessments in this chapter. Included in the classroom assessments considered in the chapter will be tests created by one teacher as well as tests created by groups of teachers from a single school or from the same school district. Overburdened classroom teachers often need to collaborate when generating suitable classroom assessments.

Although classroom assessments are not—as is true with standardized tests—administered, scored, and interpreted in a standard, predetermined fashion, they could be. That is, if educators in a certain school or district wished to do so, classroom tests could be administered, scored, and interpreted with varying degrees of standardization. But, then, we'd be dealing with standardized classroom tests, and most of the issues that were addressed in the previous chapter regarding standardized tests would all be applicable. During recent years, we have seen the emergence of "common" classroom assessments that have been constructed collaboratively by groups of teachers. If these common assessments are administered and scored in a standard manner, their usage borders on what we think of when describing standardized tests. Nonetheless, we will chiefly be dealing in this chapter with what we ordinarily think of when we refer to "teacher-made" tests.

The kinds of classroom assessments that can be employed to collect evidence of a teacher's quality are typically designed to measure students' knowledge and/or their mastery of cognitive skills. As an example of the sort of language arts *knowledge* we might want to measure, we could assess whether students can "recall and understand" the most commonly employed conventions (rules) governing punctuation and grammatical usage in written compositions. An example of the kind of *cognitive skill* that might be assessed in such tests would be a student's ability to arrive rapidly at *reasonable* mental estimates regarding the likely outcomes of diverse mathematical operations.

The varieties of items that might be used in classroom assessments include all of testing's "usual suspects," namely, multiple-choice items, two-choice items, short-answer items, and extended-response items.

Indeed, as long as the assessment techniques being employed will yield results from which valid inferences can be drawn about student growth, a wide variety of less traditional assessment ploys are eligible for use as classroom tests. For example, oral assessments or collaborative student-group tasks could certainly be used. What's most crucial is that any classroom-assessment tactics chosen should elicit students' performances from which valid inferences can be made about a teacher's ability to promote students' learning. Although the vast majority of classroom assessments focus on measuring students' cognitive growth, in Chapter 8 we will also consider how teachers might collect evidence about students' *affective growth* such as changes in students' attitudes, interests, and values.

A Quest for Evidence of Student Growth

Because of the federally spurred need for teacher evaluators to measure students' *growth* rather than merely assessing students' *status,* at least two administrations of a classroom assessment are necessary if students' performances on these assessments are to play a meaningful role in appraising teachers. Thus, some version of a pretest and posttest data-gathering design must be employed when collecting any evidence of students' growth that's to be used as an indication of what students have learned from a teacher. These pretests and posttests, however, need not be administered at the very beginning of a school year (or semester) and at the very end of a school year (or semester). Instead, classroom assessments might be given to a teacher's students before and after a given unit of instruction such as a multi-week social studies unit dealing with "How a Bill Becomes a Law." Thus, evidence of student growth might be collected for an entire school year by using pretests and posttests covering all of the year's instructional emphases. But evidence of student growth might also be collected in smaller chunks by using pretests and posttests to measure the impact of more abbreviated segments of instruction.

In the previous chapter we saw that, when collecting evidence of student growth, many teachers can compare their students' performances on *this year's* end-of-school state accountability tests with those students' performances on *last year's* end-of-school state accountability tests. Such contrasts are possible because, at certain grade levels and in certain subjects, almost all of a given teacher's students must take this year's accountability tests and also will have completed the previous year's accountability tests. Moreover, the curricular emphases in adjacent grades are often quite similar.

In many subjects and at many grade levels, however, no previous-year's test results are available for a teacher's students. What this means, simply put, is that for more than half of the nation's teachers, it will be necessary for a teacher to collect *both* pre-instruction and post-instruction evidence of students' status. If two or more tests must be administered at different times to ascertain students' growth, then use of a basic pre-instruction versus post-instruction assessment design such as that seen in Figure 5.1 will be required. In essence, what happens when we review the results of such pre-instruction versus post-instruction assessment designs is that we subtract students' pretest performances from their posttest performance, then conclude that the resulting difference (hopefully, a positive difference) is attributable to the teacher's instructional efforts.

Formative and Summative Applications

When considering the appropriateness of employing classroom assessments to collect evidence of a teacher's effectiveness, an important issue to keep in mind is whether the results of such classroom assessment ought to be used *summatively* or *formatively.* In general, when classroom assessments are employed formatively, their results are used by teachers and/or students to make decisions about whether to make adjustments in whatever they're doing. That is, results from classroom assessments, if used formatively, can help teachers decide whether they need to make any adjustments in their ongoing instructional activities. Similarly, results from such classroom assessments, if used formatively, can help students decide whether they need to make adjustments in their learning tactics, that is, changes in the ways they are trying to learn things. Formative

Figure 5.1   A Classic Pre-Instruction Versus Post-Instruction Assessment Design for Determining Student Growth

assessment should be regarded as a process in which students' performances on classroom assessments contribute to teachers' or students' adjustment decisions. This formative usage of classroom-assessment data has been treated elsewhere (Popham, 2008, 2011; Wiliam, 2011). Happily, solid research evidence now exists showing us that when formative assessment is properly employed, its beneficial impact on students' learning is remarkable (Black & Wiliam, 1998; Heritage, 2013; Wiliam, 2011).

In contrast, when classroom assessment results are employed *summatively*, they have traditionally been used to assign grades to students. However, another summative application of students' test results is to indicate the degree to which a teacher has successfully promoted student growth. In a very direct sense, then, formative uses of classroom-assessment results are improvement oriented, but summative uses of classroom-assessment results are evaluation oriented.

Most teacher evaluators who employ classroom-assessment data in their work recognize that it is essentially impossible to use a given set of classroom-assessment results *simultaneously* to fulfill both a summative and formative function. In order to maximize the instructional implications of classroom-assessment data, making those results play an evaluative role often limits their instructional-improvement yield. Such limits arise because, when assessment results are to be used summatively (such as for grading students or for evaluating teachers), what's invariably sought is an optimization of students' test performances—high-quality performances containing as few mistakes as possible. Yet, for a test's results to be most useful formatively, it is often necessary to isolate the nature of students' confusions, so the push for mistake-free test performances can actually mask where it is that students most need instructional support.

To be most effective formatively, classroom assessments must often be built to provide diagnostic insights about a student's shortcomings—even if the quest for such diagnostic data can lead to students' making "weakness-illuminating" errors. Conversely, when using classroom-assessment results summatively to illuminate evaluative judgments about a teacher's prowess, it is often necessary to establish procedures that, in order to heighten evaluative objectivity, will minimize the formative payoffs from a set of classroom-assessment results. Accordingly, when classroom-assessment evidence has been chosen to help determine a teacher's quality, as indicated in Chapter 1, it makes sense to keep separate the formative and summative applications of classroom assessment. Although, based on a bevy of research evidence, the instructional yield of the formative-assessment process is beneficial to students' learning, the collection of classroom-assessment data *for purposes of evaluating teachers* should be restricted to the summative utilization of such data.

Enhancing the Quality of Classroom-Assessment Evidence

For just a moment, let's review why it is we might wish to employ classroom assessments to assemble data that, along with other evidence, could help us arrive at an accurate judgment about a particular teacher's competence. As is the case with all of the possible evidence sources we will be reviewing in this five-chapter focus on potential teacher-evaluation evidence, we need to determine whether each source of evidence should be incorporated in a teacher-evaluation process that, in the end, will help us accurately ascertain the effectiveness of a specific teacher.

Now, let's look at classroom-assessment evidence through the prism of a particular evaluative criterion, namely, a teacher's *instructional ability*. In short, let's see whether classroom assessments should be chosen to collect their share of evidence for use in a teacher-evaluation program focused on instructional ability. We'll consider not only the wisdom of using classroom assessments in this manner, but also how those assessments should be crafted if their evaluative utility is to be optimized.

Evidence of a Teacher's Instructional Ability

For openers, we need to deal head-on with the most compelling reason we're likely to need classroom assessments to help us evaluate a teacher's instructional ability. This reason, a whopper indeed, is that for most teachers in America's schools, other than students' scores on classroom tests, there is no other credible evidence attesting to a teacher's ability to promote students' learning. That's right; although the passage of NCLB spurred the administration of annual statewide standardized accountability tests at grades 3–8 and once in high school, those accountability tests only measure students' status in mathematics and reading (as well as in writing if a state's educational officials wish to include writing in their NCLB assessments). Teachers who teach nontested grades or subjects, that is, grades or subjects in which students don't take required accountability tests, will typically have no access to state-supplied evidence of student growth for their students.

And even the teachers in grades 3–8, those teachers whose students must complete statewide NCLB tests in math and language arts, are still responsible for teaching their students in other subjects such as social studies and fine arts. Do we really intend to evaluate a teacher who teaches four or five subjects on the basis of students' test performances from only two subjects? To provide a full picture of such teachers' skills, we will often need to rely on classroom assessments even in the so-called "tested grades."

While, in a handful of states, efforts are currently underway to provide state-generated *end-of-course tests* for many subjects and for many grade levels not otherwise addressed by state accountability tests, it seems too early in the game to know if these ambitious course-focused test-development efforts will prove successful. Merely because someone sets out to create a course-specific collection of tests does not mean that those tests are going to provide accurate evidence bearing on the quality of students' learning in a specific course. (It is far more difficult to create acceptable end-of-course tests than is widely recognized.) Sadly, many of these state-developed, end-of-course tests may need to be sent directly to the paper shredder. They simply are not good enough to employ in the evaluation of teachers. Although such end-of-course tests should surely be pilot-tested before being used to evaluate a state's teachers, in some states these home-grown tests are being employed to appraise teachers without ever having been seriously tried out.

Moreover, although in a few states we can find accountability tests in other subjects and at other grade levels, the hard fact is that if we truly wish to make student growth a significant factor in a state's teacher-evaluation program (and, thereby, ensure the state's compliance with federal preferences), there is simply no other way of getting a sensible fix on students' learning. If any kind of meaningful evidence of students' learning is going to be incorporated in a program intended to evaluate all of a state's teachers, especially those teachers responsible for nontested grades and subjects, then classroom-assessment evidence must ultimately become a prominent assessment option to be used when evaluating many teachers. At this moment, and especially given the instructional insensitivity of most states' current standardized accountability tests, there is really no alternative.

Even in situations where state-level accountability tests are administered to teachers' students at certain grade levels and, as a consequence, some standardized-test results will be available for teacher-evaluation purposes, it may still make sense to buttress such standardized-test data with evidence of students' performances on additional teacher-generated classroom assessments.

So, both in settings where no other evidence of a teacher's instructional ability is going to be available, as well as in settings where students' standardized-test scores might be augmented by supplemental data from classroom assessments, classroom tests can often supply on-target evidence regarding a teacher's instructional ability. In essence, we will be judging how well a teacher *can teach* based on how well a teacher *has taught.*

The straightforward pretest/posttest data-gathering model seen earlier in Figure 5.1 represents the most intuitively understandable way to get at evidence of a teacher's ability to help students learn. And, as noted earlier, this pre-instruction to post-instruction paradigm can be employed when covering the duration of a total semester or a school year, but it can also be used in a more piecemeal manner on several separate occasions—each of which cover, say, several weeks' worth or several months' worth of instruction. Those separate pre-instruction to post-instruction contrasts, then, can be amalgamated into a more comprehensive, assessment-based estimate of a teacher's instructional ability.

Clearly, because the illustrative focus of this chapter is on a teacher's instructional ability, then our attention should be given to what a student has learned as a consequence of a teacher's instructional efforts. Fortunately for the human species, our children can learn on their own. Children can learn at home, and they can learn in many places other than school. But what we need to do is create assessments, and administer those evidence-gathering assessments in such a way that we can arrive at a valid inference about whether a particular teacher apparently was able, *because of the teacher's instructional efforts,* to enhance students' learning. This is substantially easier to say than to do. It is distressingly difficult to find out what students have learned in school because of a teacher's efforts versus finding out what those students have learned elsewhere. Try as hard as we can, we've been unable to prevent children from learning things when they're not in school. Thankfully.

What's Assessed

When determining the evidential weight, for purposes of teacher evaluation, that we might assign to students' performances on classroom assessments, one of our most important considerations should always be *what is being assessed*. If classroom-assessment results indicate that students have learned really worthwhile things, then such results should obviously be given more evidential weight than if classroom-assessment results reflect students' mastery of something trivial. Moreover, the more *instructional time* that's been devoted to promoting students' mastery of whatever is being assessed, then the more importance we should typically give to what's been assessed.

In many instances a teacher who's working with students at a particular grade, and in a particular subject, will find that the curricular targets for the teacher's students will already have been specified at the state or district level. Suppose, for instance, that in Subject X at Grade Y, a half-dozen demanding curricular aims have been officially designated for students' mastery by state authorities. In such an instance, it seems reasonable that many of a teacher's classroom assessments ought to be aimed at measuring students' achievement of those state-stipulated curricular targets. Moreover, because the Common Core State Standards have now become officially approved by many states, and when these curricular standards become better understood by those states' educators, we would expect that the curricular aims embodied in these widely endorsed content standards might well serve as the focus for teachers' before-instruction and after-instruction classroom tests.

It is difficult to argue with the proposition that if a teacher's classroom assessments measure students' mastery of truly worthwhile curricular outcomes, the results of those assessments should be regarded as more important than should the results of classroom assessments measuring less lofty curricular targets. Similarly, for students' performances on classroom assessments to play a prominent role in the evaluation of a teacher, those classroom assessments should be measuring the official knowledge and skills approved by a state's educational policymakers.

And it is at this point that we now come face-to-face with an important reality in the evaluation of teachers. Almost everyone wants to be regarded as successful. When being evaluated, we all want to be evaluated positively. This desire for positive appraisals is present whether it's a teacher who's instructing second graders or an author who's trying to write a book about teacher evaluation. It's just human nature. We want to be winners rather than losers. Accordingly, teachers will soon realize that if they are going to be evaluated, at least in part, on the basis of evidence from classroom tests showing how much growth their students have made, then it will usually be far easier to promote student growth when whatever growth that's to be assessed is based on trifling rather than challenging curricular outcomes.

Thus, we immediately recognize that the assignment of evidential weight to pre-instruction versus post-instruction results from a teacher's classroom assessments must depend heavily on judgments regarding the worth of what's being assessed. Recalling Chapter 3's description of a weighted-evidence judgmental approach to teacher evaluation, you can readily see that when weighting the evaluative significance of a teacher's classroom-assessment data, that is, when deciding on the appropriate evidential weight to be assigned to students' assessment results, not only must teacher evaluators look at pretest-to-posttest changes, but those evaluators must also make judgments about the curricular worth of what was being assessed (that is, what was being taught). After all, it does not take a full school year for a third grader to learn how to spell *dog* or *cat*.

If classroom evidence is chosen as a legitimate source for helping us get a fix on a teacher's instructional ability, and it seems unlikely that classroom-assessment evidence of student growth should ever be completely overlooked as such a source, then a two-step process might be installed for use by teacher evaluators. Such teacher evaluators should not only focus on the magnitude of students' learning (typically by relying on some version of a pretest-posttest data-gathering design), but those evaluators must also attend to the curricular importance of what was being taught and, consequently, what was being measured.

The Traditional Psychometric Triplets

In the preceding chapter you saw that when the suitability of particular standardized tests is being determined, we routinely look for evidence bearing on the time-honored factors of reliability, validity, and absence of bias. Clearly, greater evidential weight should be given to a classroom test if the test (1) is reliable, (2) is accompanied by validity evidence supporting whatever test-based inference is going to be made, and (3) can demonstrate that a solid effort has been made to reduce the test's assessment bias. Now, how much evidence in support of each of these three traditional indicators of test quality is a typical teacher realistically likely to generate regarding the teacher's own classroom tests?

Few teachers today are blessed with so much discretionary time that, merely to keep their hands busy and their brain cells humming, they will set out to seriously verify the psychometric adequacy of their own classroom assessments. Surely, even if teachers decide to study the technical virtues of their own classroom tests, most teachers are unlikely to tackle the psychometric scrutiny of their tests with the level of rigor typically required when scrutinizing standardized testing's reliability, validity, and absence of bias. More likely, a typical teacher will have no time at all to devote to the assembly of evidence regarding the traditional indices of a classroom test's quality. This is altogether understandable.

However, it should be apparent that because evidence regarding reliability, validity, and assessment bias is clearly pertinent to the evaluative confidence that we can assign to a given classroom test's results, it may well be that some teachers will find themselves able to compile at least a mild evidence regarding the technical caliber of their own teacher-made classroom tests. Here's how a few nuggets of such evidence might be collected.

With respect to reliability, one of the more important indicators of a test's consistency stems from the degree to which a test's results are stable over time. This sort of test-retest evidence deals with a kind of test consistency referred to as *stability reliability*. To get at least some evidence bearing on a test's stability reliability, if a pretest or posttest has been administered to a total class of students, perhaps a small group of those students (say, 5–10) could simply be asked to re-take the same test a day or two after they had completed the original test. The performances of this small sample of students on these two testing occasions could be contrasted in order to provide a modest indication of a classroom test's reliability (of the stability sort). While not supplying the sort of resplendent reliability evidence sought by engineers when determining a spaceship's suitability for interstellar travel, or even the kinds of reliability evidence we often see collected for nationally standardized tests, such small-scale glimpses of a classroom assessment's reliability would indicate that those collecting classroom-assessment evidence of a teacher's quality are not oblivious of the importance of measuring students' status with some degree of consistency.

Regarding validity, perhaps the most important kind of validity evidence for classroom assessments is what's referred to as *content-related evidence of validity*. This sort of evidence attempts to identify the degree to which a test's items satisfactorily represent the content represented in the inferences to be based on test-takers' scores. To assemble such evidence, a teacher might ask a small group of friends or colleagues to judge whether the test's items are in alignment with the skills or bodies of knowledge supposedly being assessed. Again, this would be a task that might be carried out by asking a panel of fellow teachers, particularly teachers who are not intimidated by the subject matter involved, to not only rate (on anonymously completed rating forms) the significance of what the test assesses, but also to rate the degree to which *each item* on the test accurately contributes to the particular score-based inference to be made. In this instance, the score-based inference at issue is whether changes in students' pretest-to-posttest scores are attributable, at least in part, to the instructional ability of those students' teacher. Although there are other, more exotic ways of assembling validity evidence for classroom assessments, this modest panel-judgment method of assembling content-related validity evidence will usually be sufficient.

Because the inference-at-issue deals with a teacher's instructional ability, the same concerns about a classroom test's instructional sensitivity arise as were seen with standardized tests in the previous chapter. One way for teachers to tackle this issue is to ask themselves, for every item on their classroom tests, the following question: "If I have taught my students with reasonable effectiveness to master the curricular aim (that is, the knowledge or skill) on which this item is based, is it likely that a substantial majority of my students will answer the item correctly?" Teachers can entice a colleague to review the items with a similar question such as, "If a teacher has taught the content standard on which this item is based, and done so with reasonable competence, will most of the teacher's students get the item right?" Clearly, this sort of item-by-item review is intended to rid a test of items for which students' correct answers might be attributable to students' socioeconomic status or inherited academic aptitudes rather than to a teacher's instructional skill. Items that appear to be instructionally insensitive should, of course, be repaired or removed from the test.

Finally, in the assembly of evidence regarding absence of bias, here's where the breadth of a teacher's friendships come in. If, for the students being taught, a teacher can persuade one or more fellow teachers who represent the same racial, ethnic, or religious groups as the students being assessed, then these colleagues can be asked to review the teacher's classroom tests to see if there are any items that might offend or unfairly penalize students from such groups. Granted that asking only a handful of teachers to review the items on a classroom assessment is far short of what one might prefer, but in view of teachers' limited free time, it is better to collect item-by-item evidence about assessment bias from even *one* fellow teacher than to collect none at all.

Again, the likelihood of a teacher's finding time to assemble classroom-assessment evidence related to reliability, validity, and assessment bias is staggeringly small. Yet, if it is possible for a teacher to undertake a psychometric appraisal of the teacher's classroom tests *without a concomitant loss of the teacher's sanity,* such an appraisal of classroom assessments will help teacher evaluators who must determine how much evidential weight to give students' performances on a teacher's classroom assessments.

If teachers need guidelines regarding how best to carry out these sorts of psychometric appraisals of their own classroom assessments, suggestions for doing so can be found in almost any textbook designed to be used in courses for prospective/practicing teachers dealing with classroom assessment (for example, see McMillan, 2010; Popham, 2014).

Following Test Development, Improvement, and Scoring Rules

For all of the most commonly employed types of test items that are routinely used in classroom assessments, a set of *item-development rules* and *item-improvement rules* exist. These rules can be found in almost every educational measurement textbook that's ever been written. Over the years, these rules have been identified, refined, and expanded on by the writers of these measurement textbooks.

These widely accepted test-building and test-improving guidelines come to us from two sources. First, there are rules drawn from actual research investigations in which different item-structure variations have been studied. For example, multiple-choice items featuring three, four, and five answer-choices might be contrasted to see which answer-choice option seems most effective. Many of today's test-development rules can trace their origins to such empirical studies. Most of the rules, however, come to us from the documented experiences of those individuals over the years who have written literally thousands of the sorts of items most likely to be found in teachers' classroom tests.

If teachers follow the item-development rules for classroom tests found in almost any textbook dealing with educational testing, their resulting classroom assessments are likely to be better than the classroom assessments constructed by teachers who have no conversance with the "dos and don'ts" of how to build classroom tests. Better classroom tests, of course, are more likely to yield evidence better supporting the validity of inferences about teachers' instructional ability.

In addition to a powerful set of *test-development* rules, similar sets of rules exist for *test improvement*. Easy-to-use techniques exist to ferret out shortcomings in, for example, short-answer items, extended-response items, or multiple-choice items after those items have once been written and used with students. Simple empirical techniques, rarely involving mathematical manipulations beyond multiplying and dividing, are presented in all classroom-assessment textbooks (for instance, Popham, 2014; Stiggins & Chappuis, 2012).

Beyond the routine guidelines for *constructing* and *improving* classroom tests, educational measurement textbooks also contain many helpful rules to follow when *scoring* students' responses to classroom assessments. When attempting to enhance the validity of test-based inferences about teachers' instructional abilities, it is definitely advantageous to adhere to these scoring guidelines dealing with such topics as the development and use of rubrics (scoring guides) when evaluating students' answers to constructed-response items. Properly scored classroom assessments, as is all too obvious, will yield teacher-evaluation evidence much more useful than will improperly scored classroom assessments.

Clearly, greater evidential weight should always be given to students' performances on tests that have been built in accord with the rules of item-writing as well as the rules for test-improving. These rules are easy to understand, and really far less trouble to apply than might be thought. When students' performances on classroom assessments arrive after reliance on these sorts of test-developing and test-polishing rules, those performances should almost always be given more evidential weight than students' performance on classroom tests constructed without reliance on such rules.

Looking back, then, we have considered three factors to employ when strengthening teacher-evaluation evidence based on students' performances on teachers' classroom assessment. First, those assessments should measure students' attainment of truly commendable skills and/or knowledge. Second, evidence bearing on reliability, validity, and absence of bias can provide an idea about the quality of the assessment instruments themselves. Finally, if classroom assessments are built in accord with the widely available rules for constructing, improving, and scoring students' responses to classroom assessments, we can usually place greater confidence in the resultant evidence obtained by the use of those classroom assessments.

HAVE TEACHERS PLAYED IT STRAIGHT?

Several paragraphs ago, it was suggested that because teachers (and all other human beings) wish to be regarded positively, there is always the possibility that an approval-seeking teacher might aim instructionally at lower-level, more readily attainable curricular targets. To verify that teachers are not committing such a sin against evaluative accuracy, it was suggested that a review panel could consider teacher-submitted evidence regarding the appropriateness of the curricular targets being measured by the teacher's classroom assessments. If no such evidence has been submitted regarding the worthiness of what's being measured by a teacher's classroom tests, then teacher evaluators may need to collect their own evidence to make sure that a teacher's students are not demonstrating substantial "growth" merely because the teacher was pursuing indefensibly low curricular aims. Student-growth evidence obtained from classroom assessments measuring high-level curricular aims should, as noted earlier, surely count for more than should evidence drawn from classroom assessments measuring students' achievement of inconsequential outcomes.

But there's a second, serious evaluative concern when teacher evaluators rely on classroom-assessment evidence of student growth to reflect a teacher's instructional ability. To illustrate, here's a fictional scenario for you to consider. Suppose an experienced principal was considering how much evaluative weight to assign to a set of very impressive pretest-to-posttest improvements displayed by Teacher Z's students as they demonstrated their mastery of a particularly high-level cognitive skill in mathematics on teacher-made classroom tests. Although on a pretest, Teacher Z's students had, on average, scored at about 40% correct when the test was administered at the beginning of the semester, when the same test was re-administered several months later at the end of the semester, all students' average scores were at least 90% correct or higher. In fact, almost half of Teacher Z's students earned posttest scores of 100% correct on the end-of-semester test! Now, if you were our fictional principal assigned to judge the instructional ability of Teacher Z, how much evaluative weight would you assign to this classroom-assessment evidence? Would you assign to this teacher's classroom-assessment evidence *much, medium,* or *microscopic* evidential weight?

Now, keeping in mind your original assignment of evidential weight to this evidence, how might the following information influence your weight-assignment decision? Suppose it came to your attention that, for almost an entire semester, Teacher Z's students had been required, almost daily, to discuss each item on the test, one item at a time, to distinguish between correct and incorrect answers. Teacher Z, when asked about this practice, indicated that he believed an item-by-item "forensic analysis" was the best way for his students to understand what was actually going on in each of the test's items. When asked if such intensified attention to the test's items would interfere with conclusions about student growth based on an analysis of pretest-to-posttest results, Teacher Z replied, "Don't we want our students to master the key cognitive skills of mathematics? And doesn't this classroom test supply legitimate evidence regarding how well a student has learned the specific skill that's being measured?"

Now, based on this new information about Teacher Z's instructional approach, how would you weight the evaluative significance of the remarkable pre-instruction to post-instruction gains seen for Teacher Z's students?

Hopefully, you would dramatically decrease whatever evidential weight you had originally given to this classroom-assessment evidence. Teacher Z was simply "teaching to the test's items" by excessively familiarizing his students with the innards of each item.

Such item-focused instruction essentially destroys the validity of any score-based inferences about this teacher's instructional ability. If the mathematical skill being taught and measured is, indeed, a cognitive skill that students should master, then students' performances on an *item-taught* test give us no accurate insights regarding whether students can actually use this allegedly "mastered" math skill when tackling items with which those students are not already familiar. Any item-focused teaching clearly erodes the validity of inferences about a teacher's instructional ability based on students' assessment performances.

How then, do we cope with what may be an understandable, although unattractive, inclination of certain teachers? As usual, we need to assemble evidence that teachers have *not* engaged in serious item-focused teaching related to any classroom assessments being employed for teacher-evaluation purposes. As an example of such "straight-shooter evidence," an administrator or another teacher can, immediately following the administration of a posttest, distribute to a teacher's students a set of brief, anonymously completed inventories asking about the extent to which those students have received instruction dealing specifically with the test items just completed—not instruction dealing with these *kinds* of items but, instead, instruction focused on *the particular items* that were used in a test.

Another way to enhance the persuasiveness of classroom-assessment evidence is to make certain that students' test performances have been *accurately and honestly scored*. In the case of scoring selected-response items, such as those used in true-false tests or in multiple-choice tests, scoring of students' performance is reasonably straightforward. However, when classroom assessments incorporate any sort of constructed-response items such as essay items or short-answer items, then teachers can usually enhance the credibility of their classroom-assessment data by having the tests scored not only by themselves but, in addition, by having students' responses blind-scored by colleagues, parents, or other members of the community. Students' *undated* pretests and posttests can be coded, then mixed together so the blind scorers do not know whether each scored student's response had been completed prior to or following instruction. After the blind-scoring has been concluded, then students' responses could be reassigned to their pretest or posttest categories so that contrasts can be made between students' pre-instruction and post-instruction levels of performance.

Clearly, to heighten the evaluative influence of students' performances on classroom assessments, care must be taken to (1) ensure the accuracy with which classroom assessments are scored, (2) counteract criticisms that teachers have succumbed to self-interest by distorting the scoring of students' classroom tests, and (3) avoid any behavior that would be perceived by others to distort the evaluative worth of classroom-assessment evidence. If teachers can, themselves, supply information attesting to the accuracy and objectivity with which their students' performances on classroom tests have been scored, greater confidence can be placed on the evaluative influence of such evidence.

What is being sought, clearly, is evidence bearing on the credibility of classroom-assessment evidence related to a teacher's instructional ability, as represented by the pretest-to-posttest progress of the teacher's students. If both the teachers who are being evaluated, and the teacher evaluators who are doing the judging, recognize the importance of supplying evidence confirming the indisputable accuracy of evaluative inferences based on classroom-assessment evidence, then we can usually arrive at a more accurate assignment of evidential weight to this form of teacher-evaluation evidence.

It may seem intimidating to recognize the presence of many threats that might reduce the evaluative usefulness of classroom-assessment data, and to realize that genuine attention to these threats must be undertaken if we wish to rely seriously on such evidence when evaluating teachers. But let's not get so caught up with "the things to avoid and the things to do" that we overlook the fundamental reason we even consider the use of classroom-assessment data when evaluating teachers. To arrive at a judgment regarding a teacher's instructional ability, we obviously need evidence regarding how well a teacher can instruct. Because classroom assessments can capture students' learning closer to its occurrence than can any other evidence of such learning, then this evidence should be a powerful illuminator of how well a teacher can actually teach.

Classroom-assessment evidence, if collected with care, can supply useful evaluative evidence to appraise teachers. But if classroom-assessment evidence is to be taken seriously by teacher evaluators, such evidence must be *credible,* that is, must be accompanied by information attesting to the accuracy and believability of the evidence. Because teachers will be the primary evidence collectors of this kind of evidence, it is imperative that the evidence is seen not as self-serving but, rather, as an accurate illuminator of a teacher's quality.

EVIDENTIAL-WEIGHT GUIDELINES

What we need to do when considering the use of classroom-assessment evidence, then, is try to minimize the factors that reduce the validity of inferences about a teacher's instructional competence, while maximizing the factors that enhance the validity of those inferences. If you were an assistant principal, designated as your school's summative evaluator, who was trying to decide how much weight to assign to classroom-assessment evidence, what you would need to do is *use your common sense.* Collect, score, and analyze students' results on classroom tests so that, even if you were a thoroughgoing skeptic regarding the evaluative yield of classroom-assessment data, you'd still be persuaded by the evidence at hand. Either teacher evaluators, or teachers themselves, should identify any obvious credibility weaknesses in the classroom-assessment evidence being collected, and then set out to fix them.

- Greater evidential weight should be given to students' performances on classroom assessments measuring those students' mastery of truly commendable curricular aims.
- Greater evidential weight should be given to classroom-assessment results when evidence is at hand supporting an assessment's reliability, validity, and absence of bias.
- Greater evidential weight should be given to students' classroom-assessment performances when the assessments have been constructed, improved, and scored in accord with accepted practices.
- Greater evidential weight should be given to classroom-assessment evidence when information is available supporting the credibility of the evidence.

CHAPTER IMPLICATIONS FOR THREE AUDIENCES

For Policymakers: Realistically, one reason the architects of federal teacher-evaluation guidelines insisted on the prominent use of students' test scores is that there is a presumption of objective accuracy linked to any evidence capable of being represented numerically. In recognition that federal officials may have, perhaps understandably, been wary of "softer" forms of teacher-evaluation evidence that might be more easily manipulated, policymakers must be especially attentive to the quality of the numerical evidence obtainable from classroom assessments. The dominant inference around which all teacher-evaluation evidence converges is, simply, "How well does this teacher teach?" As educational policymakers review the nature of any classroom-assessment evidence bearing on a teacher's instructional skill, therefore, those policymakers should be particularly attentive to the legitimacy of this evidence in determining a teacher's effectiveness. Some classroom-assessment evidence of teachers' competence will be persuasive; some will not. Policymakers need to know which is which.

For Administrators: Administrators, particularly school-site administrators, sit squarely astride the place where classroom-assessment evidence of teachers' skill is born. An assessment-knowledgeable school administrator, then, can have a powerful role in enhancing the meaningfulness of any classroom-assessment evaluative evidence collected in that administrator's school. Here is another moment, then, when a school-site administrator's grasp of fundamental concepts and procedures of educational assessment must surely be solid. If not, then that administrator needs to engage in some personal professional development focused on assessment—especially classroom assessment. Moreover, beyond the usual nuts and bolts of assessment featured in most measurement textbooks, administrators will definitely need to assist a school's teachers in devising procedures ensuring the perceived accuracy of teacher-collected evidence of students' classroom performance. Such guidelines will not be found in traditional measurement texts, but the importance of assessment credibility cannot be overemphasized these days. Administrators, district and school-site, will need to deal with some previously untreated issues to help teachers collect accurate and credible classroom-assessment data. Today's educational administrators, therefore, definitely need to know their assessment onions.

For Teachers: Because, in almost all cases, classroom-assessment evidence will be collected by teachers themselves, it is apparent that many teachers will need to bolster their understandings about the sorts of classroom evidence that provide compelling insights regarding a teacher's instructional ability. Let's be candid: If a state's annual accountability tests are instructionally insensitive—as is the case in most states—then most teachers' most accurate evidence of their instructional ability will, of necessity, come from the teacher's own classroom assessments. Yet, teachers not only need to construct solid classroom assessments, those teachers also need to assemble evidence attesting to the credibility of students' performances on those assessments. This pair of responsibilities, for most teachers, represents a brand-new challenge. As we saw in earlier chapters, this is another clear instance when teachers need to increase their understandings related to assessment—in this case, classroom assessment.

CHAPTER 6

Evidence From Classroom Observations

"There's no better way to determine a teacher's competence than to watch the teacher teach!" This opinion regarding how best to evaluate teachers, phrased in various ways, is almost certain to be expressed by one or more individuals whenever teacher evaluation is being discussed. After all, it makes so much common sense. That's because, if you want to evaluate how well someone can do Thing X, what you need to do is watch that person engaging in "Thing X–doing." Thereupon, you can often tell whether the doing is dandy or dismal. And this is why, of course, whenever the evaluation of teachers is being considered, one of the most often recommended ways of determining a teacher's skill is to observe the teacher in action.

In the previous two chapters, we looked at teacher-evaluation evidence that's obtainable when students' knowledge and skills are measured by using standardized tests and classroom assessments. In this chapter we turn to another frequently employed way to evaluate teachers, namely, observations of a teacher's classroom conduct, that is, the scrutiny of what goes on while a teacher is teaching.

As suggested above, evidence of a teacher's skill that's collected by using classroom observations is laden with intuitive appeal. One reason behind the almost universal applause given to classroom observations is that most adults believe they can *personally* distinguish between good teaching and bad teaching when they see it. Rarely, therefore, are any large-scale efforts to evaluate teachers planned these days without someone's calling for the inclusion of classroom-observation evidence. Remember, when today's adults were students, they watched numerous teachers in action for many years. Those adults can usually recall one or two really stellar teachers who were wonderful, and one or two really weak teachers who were quite non-wonderful. With these sometimes vivid recollections in people's minds, should we be surprised that many individuals believe they can accurately evaluate teaching simply by watching it as it takes place?

This chapter is intended to provide you with insights regarding whether classroom observations should be used as a way of obtaining evidence bearing on a teacher's quality. Please recall that, for illustrative purposes in this and the other four chapters about potential evidence sources, we will be seeing whether a specific source of evidence can make a useful contribution to evaluating a teacher's *instructional ability.* In this chapter we'll be identifying factors to consider when teacher evaluators decide (1) *whether* to use classroom-observation evidence at all in the evaluation of a teacher and, if so, (2) *how to weight* particular versions of whatever classroom-observation evidence has been collected.

In addition, we'll take a serious look at two widely used frameworks currently being employed as key features of several states' teacher-evaluation systems, namely, the observation frameworks devised by Charlotte Danielson and by Robert Marzano. When classroom observations are being used in many of today's teacher-appraisal systems, the Danielson or Marzano conceptualizations, sometimes modified, have often been chosen for the collection of observational data to evaluate teachers. As a consequence, those who wish to appraise and, if necessary, to improve an extant teacher-evaluation system should have at least a nodding acquaintance with the Danielson and Marzano approaches. Fortunately, several excellent explanatory resources developed by these two scholars are available for those who wish to dive more deeply into these methods of observing teachers in action.

WHAT'S DISTINCTIVE
ABOUT CLASSROOM OBSERVATIONS?

In the world of real estate, a popular truth-capturing maxim is that, when placing a value on a particular property, what must be considered is "location, location, location!" Well, in the world of teacher evaluation, a maxim—though cited less often than it should be—is "terminology, terminology, terminology!" If teacher evaluators are sloppy with the language they use to label what they are up to, it will not take long before "what they are up to" becomes misunderstood and, as a consequence, misused. This is certainly the case with classroom observations and the evidence they can supply. Accordingly, let's make our descriptive labels about observations both crisp and clear. We can start by drawing an especially significant distinction between the evidence of a teacher's quality that's supplied by *observations* and the evidence that's supplied by *ratings.*

Observations Versus Ratings

Ratings of a teacher's effectiveness are typically supplied by an administrator in the teacher's school. Usually, the administrator providing these ratings is the school's principal, but in larger schools such ratings are often dispensed by an assistant principal or, possibly, by a department head. Here's where confusion in labeling usually arises. This is because these school-site administrators often arrive at their conclusions regarding a teacher's competence by drawing on various kinds of evaluative evidence—only one of which is obtained from classroom observations. For instance, an assistant principal might make a judgment about a teacher's quality based, at least in part, on private discussions with the teacher about the merits of different instructional tactics, or by the teacher's comments during faculty meetings regarding the most effective ways to motivate students. An administrator might also have heard from parents about the positive (or negative) interactions they experienced with the teacher who is being evaluated. And, then, there is the willingness of a teacher to pitch in when a school's extracurricular activities take place. School administrators think more positively about teachers who "do their bit" in making a school work. In short, when a school administrator rates the effectiveness of a teacher, even though one of the contributions to the administrator's rating might have been provided by the administrator's observations of the teacher's teaching, ratings often are based on more sources of information than observations. When educators use the label "observations" interchangeably with "ratings," they display the sort of verbal imprecision that's apt to engender a confused way of thinking about key aspects of teacher evaluation.

All right, if ratings aren't observations, then what is it that's involved when teacher evaluators collect evidence of a teacher's skill by using classroom observations? In this book, the following definition of classroom observations, when used for teacher evaluation, will be employed:

> *Classroom-observation evaluative evidence refers to systematically collected data by trained observers who employ a formal observation instrument to ascertain a teacher's use of designated behaviors, the quality of such usage being determined during the observation or thereafter.*

Let's look for a moment at the key ingredients in this definition. When considering the definition, you will note that we are dealing with *systematically* collected data, not casually collected evidence that might be available because an observer happened to visit a teacher's class for a half an hour or, perhaps, strolled through a classroom for a few minutes. In addition, the observers must have been *trained* to collect observation data. Later in the chapter, we will see that the duration and quality of such training can vary substantially. Moreover, there's a *formal observation instrument* to be used, not merely an observer's watching what happens in class, and then jotting down a few notes on scratch paper about notable classroom events. Observation instruments, sometimes oft-revised ones, should also be used by classroom observers. Moreover, what's on those observation forms, that is, the set of factors to be observed, usually determine the meaningfulness of the classroom-observation evidence that's been collected.

Finally, please recognize in the foregoing definition that, in order for classroom-observation evidence to be used when evaluating teachers, the *quality* of what's going on in class needs to be identified. With certain observation procedures, these quality designations are made "on the spot." For example, the observer assigns a numerical quantity of, say, 1 to 4 points, to each of the factors included on the observation instrument being used. The more points that are assigned, the more effectively the observer thinks the teacher is employing the observation form's dimensions. Using such forms, a total score can be calculated immediately for an observed teacher.

With other observation instruments, however, the observer simply notes the presence or absence of certain behaviors by the teacher, for instance, whether a teacher allows reasonable "wait time" before demanding responses from students. Later, these

use/non-use frequencies can be summarized and assigned evaluative designations so that a teacher's "Use of Effective Discussion
Tactics" might be designated as *superior, acceptable,* or *unaccept-
able.* Ultimately, when using classroom observations to evaluate
teachers, the data collected during an evaluation must be transformed into some qualitative representation (for instance, by using
a numerical scale or choosing among evaluative categories) that
can contribute directly to the evaluation of a particular teacher.

Playing the Odds: Observation of Instructional Means

To grasp the potential of classroom-observation data to make a
meaningful contribution to the evaluation of a teacher, those involved
in teacher evaluation need to recognize what classroom-observation
data can tell us, and what such data can't. Fluffy thinking about what
classroom-observation data actually represent can lead to the creation of teacher-evaluation procedures that are far from defensible.

Let's deal with the issue of "evidence defensibility" as we
might if we were trying to come up with an accurate evaluation of
a teacher's *instructional ability.* Looking at instructional ability in its
most basic form, we might conclude that the ultimate way we should
evaluate a teacher's instructional ability is to determine how deftly
the teacher can promote students' learning. That's what instructional
ability is, after all, the skill of a teacher in instructing kids so that
those kids learn what they're supposed to learn. Students' learning
or, if you prefer, student growth, thus becomes the *end* by which we
determine the effectiveness of a teacher's instructional *means.* This
ends/means distinction is an especially salient one because, when
evaluating teachers, we will often be considering evidence that
illuminates a teacher's success in promoting appropriate *ends.* But
teacher evaluators often use evidence that illuminates a teacher's
success in providing appropriate *means* for accomplishing the
sought-for ends. Teacher evaluators who get mixed up when distinguishing between means and ends are careening toward confusion.

When we observe what goes on in classrooms, our focus should
be on the activities in which the teacher is engaging or, perhaps,
the activities in which students have been directed by the teacher
to engage. We are looking at instructional activities in the plausible
belief that the more appropriate are a teacher's instructional activities, the more likely it is that students' learning will take place. Let's

deal with this pivotal "likelihood" issue. It really lies at the heart of classroom observations.

Through the years, because of the findings of empirical research investigations, educators have assembled a rather impressive array of "likelihood" evidence regarding how best to teach students. For example, when teachers are trying to get students to master a particular cognitive skill, such as a student's ability to distinguish between the factual and opinion segments of a newspaper editorial, abundant empirical evidence shows us that if teachers give their students opportunities to practice making such fact-versus-opinion distinctions, and the teacher then supplies suitable feedback, especially when students err, it is *more likely* that students will master this cognitive skill than when no such practice and feedback have been supplied. Today's teachers have access to a hoard of evidence-supported findings that can lead those teachers to the use of instructional practices deemed likely to result in desired outcomes for their students. These "likely payoff" instructional activities constitute the means; students' achievement of a curricular aim represents the end, that is, the intended learning outcome.

Yet, and you might have anticipated the proverbial ointment-stuck fly that's now about to vex us: When it comes to instructional procedures, "likely payoff" is not the same as "certain payoff." That's right, Miss Lee can toss into the instruction of her fourth graders all the high-likelihood, research-ratified instructional principles she can incorporate, and yet—for reasons unfathomable—Miss Lee's students can still stumble. For example, Miss Lee's students simply aren't able to master Skill Q, a key cognitive skill they are supposed to acquire. Perhaps the problem is some aspect of Miss Lee's personality that, when subtly communicated to her students, many of those students find off-putting. Perhaps it is a deficiency in these fourth graders' understandings attributable to their third-grade teacher who not only planted the seeds of confusion in the building blocks leading up to Skill Q, but also seems to have emphatically reinforced such confusion. Whatever the factors are that are apparently messing up students' mastery of Skill Q, those factors are present. And even the impressive array of likely payoff instructional principles that Miss Lee tossed into her teaching were not able to save the day.

If we had, at our disposal, simply marvelous educational tests that could provide us with unflawed evidence from which we could arrive at wonderfully precise, super-valid, never-miss inferences about students' learning, then there would really be no need to obtain any evidence bearing on the means a teacher uses to promote students' attainment of the curricular ends being sought. After all, we'd already have our ends evidence because of those simply marvelous educational tests. But, as you know, we do not now have at hand simply marvelous educational tests providing us with super-valid, never-miss inferences about what kids have learned.

And this is why, of necessity, we must often rely on evidence garnered from watching what teachers do in the classroom to help us evaluate a teacher. Properly collected *means* evidence can help teacher evaluators arrive at an accurate evaluation of a teacher. The better the classroom-observation evidence, the more confidence we can have in the evaluative significance of such evidence.

An Observational Reality: The Mysterious Middle Group

Teacher evaluators must reckon with a reality that's soon encountered by anyone who seriously attempts to appraise teachers by observing those teachers in action. It's a commonsensical reality that might best be illustrated by a hypothetical example, followed by a serious question for you to answer. You'll find both the example and your question in the next paragraph.

Please imagine that you are a member of a research team that's been trying to devise an optimally effective observation form to use in the evaluation of 1,000 experienced teachers. The factors on which you are to observe a teacher's behavior are all based on empirically proven instructional tactics that, when used by a teacher, have a high probability of supporting students' learning. The observation form that you and your colleagues are using has been revised many times on the basis of in-the-field tryouts. You, along with the other observers in your team, have been carefully trained and, when you independently observe teachers' behaviors, you and your colleagues typically come up with a remarkably high level of inter-observer agreement about what has been seen. In short, you are an observer who's using a properly developed observation form, you've been well trained, and your observations can identify which teachers are using the proven instructional principles around which your research project is structured. Now, here's the question for you: *Given the all-around excellence of your group's approach, do you think you will be able to supply useful evaluation evidence regarding most of the 1,000 teachers you are slated to observe?*

You are, of course, free to answer the above question in any way that suits you. If, for instance, you are a glass-is-half-full sort of person, you might well supply a positive response to the italicized query. That is, you may conclude that, for most of the 1,000 teachers to be evaluated, you will be able to come up with classroom-observation evidence that will be useful. But, if that's your answer, you're probably mistaken. Bitter experience shows teacher evaluators that, even in settings where all the preparations for classroom observation simply glisten with goodness, teacher evaluators are in for a disappointment if they hope to use observational evidence to help evaluate *most* teachers.

Classroom observers in such an optimal setting can, without much difficulty, identify the *best* users of likely payoff instructional principles. Similarly, those observers can, with equal ease, identify the *worst* users of those instructional principles. Perhaps the top 10–15% and the bottom 10–15% of likely payoff principle users can be readily and unarguably identified. But after this low-hanging fruit has been plucked, a huge middle group of teachers remains—teachers who use some of the designated instructional principles, but not others. The many teachers whose level of principle usage is so similar that they simply cannot be distinguished from one another must still be evaluated—one teacher at a time. The undifferentiated observational evidence for this huge middle group often makes the evaluative contribution of observation data downright questionable for many teachers.

It is sometimes the case that when educational policymakers, or everyday citizens, are asked whether observations of a teacher's classroom instruction can provide useful evaluative evidence, their responses will be both instant and emphatically affirmative. But odds are that those positive responders are thinking about the extreme groups of teachers, that is, the easy-to-spot stellar teachers and the equally easy-to-spot ineffectual teachers. What's forgotten about is the hefty mid-quality group for which classroom observation data are far less useful.

One possible way of coping with this reality might be to increase the evaluative weight of classroom-observation evidence for extreme-group teachers, yet decrease the evaluative weight of mid-quality observational evidence. Clearly, dealing with observation-based evidence by tailoring its evaluative significance for different teachers represents a nontrivial challenge—both methodologically

and politically—for those teacher evaluators who wish to incorporate classroom-observation data in a teacher-evaluation process.

Getting the Most Evaluative Mileage
Out of Classroom-Observation Evidence

Because means are, in many instances, accurately predictive
of ends, it would be silly not to consider seriously the inclusion of
observation-based data in the array of evidence a teacher evaluator might wish to consider when evaluating a particular teacher.
Remember, because likely payoff instructional principles are based
on solid research evidence, those principles are genuinely potent. To
illustrate, if we could select at random from a state's teachers a group
of 100 teachers who fully and constantly employ research-supported
instructional principles in their teaching, and also a group of 100
teachers who rarely employ those same instructional principles,
we'd almost certainly find that the students of the 100 principle
users would have learned much better than the students of the 100
principle nonusers. Given the research evidence undergirding the
instructional principles, this is almost a certainty. But not all the students of the principle-using teachers would have learned what they
were supposed to learn. And not all of the students of the teachers
who didn't use the principles would have failed to learn what they
were supposed to learn.

Although the odds are in favor of students' learning well if
they are taught by teachers who play the instructional game with
pedagogical panache, some of those teachers' students won't learn as
much as we hope. And the converse is equally true. Yes, even if some
teachers rarely employ sound instructional principles, their students
may still learn gobs and gobs. This is why, when we decide to employ
classroom-observation data in any strategy to evaluate teachers, we
need to be confident that we've done as much as possible to make
the observation-based evidence as accurate as it can be. Here, then,
are a few ways to enhance the quality of teacher-evaluation evidence
based on classroom observations.

A large enough sample of teacher behavior. One of the very
first commandments of sensible classroom observation is that it
must be done often enough and for sufficiently long chunks of time
that the observers arrive at what is, in essence, a *representative*
picture of what usually goes on in a teacher's classroom. This sort

of observation-based gathering of evidence is akin to what happens when we try to measure students' achievement of a specific cognitive skill. If we use only a single item to assess students' skill mastery, we will have far less confidence in any test-based inference about a student's skill mastery than the confidence we would have if we had used 10 items measuring that same skill. A greater representation of the student's current skill-mastery level allows us to make test-based interpretations with more accuracy. Similarly, with respect to classroom observations, you can readily see that the larger our sample of classroom watching, the more confidence we can have in any resultant observation-based inferences about the way a teacher routinely provides instruction to students.

What is the minimum number of classroom observations, and for how long should those observations be? These are both tough questions to answer. That's because classroom observations cannot be carried out for pennies. It takes serious dollars to implement a serious classroom observation program, not only to train the observers but, even more significantly, to actually have teacher evaluators devote the hours of observation required to arrive at defensible inferences about the way teachers typically engage in instruction. Certainly, one or two visits by an observer, even a well-trained observer, will fail to provide a particularly accurate inference about the degree to which a teacher engages in certain instructional behaviors.

To illustrate, what if one of the key observational factors an observer is looking for when sitting in on a teacher's class revolves around the clarity with which a teacher lets students discern what is expected of them and, having done so, lets students know what factors will be used when students' success in meeting that expectation is to be judged? Well, if only two observations take place during a school year, and both of those observations were carried out a day *after* the teacher being observed had described the learning goals for students and the evaluative criteria that would be used to determine students' goal mastery, then the observer would never have had an opportunity to see that the teacher was, indeed, adhering totally to what was expected in the way of letting students know what's expected of them. What the observer was looking for, annoyingly, happened to take place when the observer was elsewhere. And this is why skimpy observations just don't do the job.

The importance of typicality. When evaluating teachers, classroom observations supply us with evidence—in the form of sampled behavior—of what teachers routinely do in their classrooms. As a practical matter, no states or school districts can afford to place *full-time* observers in all teachers' classrooms to observe every minute of every school day. This would require an essential doubling of the adults needed in our schools. Such staff doubling would be silly.

So, when teacher evaluators collect evidence about what a teacher does in the teacher's classroom on, say, Wednesday of the fifth week of the school year, the observation evidence collected is regarded as a sample of the teacher's typical behavior. Perhaps there will be several additional observations of the teacher's classroom behavior during the school year so that, when all of these observation results are summarized, what emerges will represent a meaningful reflection of what the teacher *usually* does instructionally.

We sample a teacher's classroom behavior, and then we infer that what we have seen during our observations is reasonably indicative of how the teacher typically tackles teaching. Putting it differently, we collect observational evidence, then infer that what we've seen during our limited visits to the teacher's classroom will be representative of how a teacher actually teaches.

And this leads us to the practical issue of whether classroom observations should be *announced* or *unannounced.* If our quest is for observation-based evidence from which accurate inferences can be made about the way a teacher typically engages in instruction, then the choice between announced and unannounced observations is unarguably clear. Although, if a classroom observation is intended for purposes of helping a teacher improve instructionally, that is, for a formative rather than for a summative function, then there can often be a productive role for announced classroom observations. For instance, suppose a teacher and the teacher's principal have collaboratively decided to focus on sharpening a teacher's classroom-management skills, and have decided that, during an agreed-on day, the principal will observe a designated class session in which the teacher attempts to employ two new classroom-management tactics the teacher and principal have been discussing. This sort of advance-notice classroom observation makes a good deal of sense for such a formative, professional-development mission. Both the teacher and the principal can deal with an instruction-related tactic that the teacher apparently needs to strengthen, and the teacher can make certain that the tactic is used during the principal's formatively focused classroom observation.

However, when the mission of classroom-observation evidence is for purposes of evaluating—not improving—a teacher, then unannounced observations are the only way to go. If, for evaluation purposes, a teacher is told that, on a specified day and at a specified time, a classroom observation will take place, then any teacher whose brain is not in siesta mode will try to do a really good instructional job during the scheduled observation session. What the observer will see is almost certainly going to be atypical. Understandably, teachers will want to do their best when an evaluation-focused observation is coming up. What the observer is apt to see, therefore, will be a show, not a typical representation of what usually transpires in the teacher's classroom. Any factors that diminish the typical nature of what an observer sees, of course, will reduce the validity of observation-based inferences about a teacher's use of the instructional procedures believed likely to enhance students' learning.

Quality of the observation instrument and its usage. If an observer attempts to record what a teacher does during a classroom session by making impromptu notes on a 3- x 5-inch index card—even using both sides—odds are that those notes won't yield a comprehensive, accurate picture of what truly went on in class. A necessary requirement of any classroom observations destined for use in evaluating teachers is that the observation data be *systematically* collected. And systematic data collection invariably requires classroom observers to rely on some sort of observation instrument to help them focus on what's regarded as most important. Later in the chapter, we'll be considering two popular observation approaches to illustrate the kinds of observation forms likely to be employed when collecting, for evaluative purposes, classroom-observation evidence.

As noted earlier, an observation form can be structured so that an observer can, upon seeing a particular occurrence in the classroom, supply an immediate evaluative judgment regarding that occurrence, that is, can assign a quality-designating number (for instance, ranging from a high of 5 to a low of 1) or a label (for instance, ranging from "Great" to "Ghastly") representing the quality of what had been observed. Alternately, an observer might simply note the frequency with which certain behaviors have occurred, and then—after the observation has been concluded—assign qualitative designations to what had been seen based on a more leisurely analysis of the collected data.

Because teaching is a remarkably complex endeavor, and varies in many ways depending on the particulars of a specific instructional context, through the years we have seen a number of observation systems devised and used in our schools, either for a summative, that is, evaluative purpose or, more often, for a formative, improvement-focused purpose. These observational guidelines typically take the form of what today's teachers refer to as *rubrics,* that is, the scoring guides educators employ when evaluating students' answers to any sort of constructed-response test items. Rubrics help test-scorers know what to focus on when they evaluate a student-generated response. Similarly, the observation forms we've seen developed through the years can help classroom observers know what to focus on when they watch a teacher in action—and how to evaluate what they've been watching.

Typically, classroom observation forms identify a series of dimensions that guide the observer's data gathering. In addition to the observation form itself, a set of guidelines usually govern the form's usage. For instance, an observer might be directed to assign an observation-based value to each of the form's dimensions only once per hour. Conversely, some researchers in the 1960s required classroom observers to render judgments almost constantly, for example, every three seconds! Clearly, the protocol for an observation form's usage can make a difference in the quality of data obtained by using that form.

What's most important about any observation instrument chosen for the collection of evaluative information, as well as the usage guidelines accompanying that instrument, is that the nature of the evidence collected is apt to provide an accurate picture of the observed teacher's instruction. If too many observational dimensions appear to be present for even well-trained observers to employ, or there seem to be too few observational dimensions to accurately represent the instruction's key elements, then we should be wary of any evaluative evidence collected via such observation instruments.

Finally, and this last requirement is particularly important, the dimensions that function as the structure for an observation instrument should be supported by as much empirical research as possible. Remember, the essence of classroom observations is to determine if a teacher's instruction adheres to the instructional precepts that, if followed, appear likely to promote students' learning. Well, clearly, the more research evidence that can be assembled in support of "Instructional Principle X," the more confidence we should have when including that dimension as a likely payoff dimension in an observation instrument. If a classroom-observation instrument is simply dreamed up by folks who stake out a set of observational dimensions supported by little empirical research, then we should give scant credence to the evidence collected when using such an observation instrument. Fortunately, the two illustrative observational approaches we will soon be considering (by Danielson and Marzano) both rest on their architects' careful analysis of research evidence supporting the use of particular instructional moves.

The caliber of observers' training. Observation instruments, if used by badly trained observers, will usually yield awful evidence. This "awful-evidence hypothesis" has been confirmed over the years by many investigators who, having invested great effort in the development of wondrous observation instruments, then fail to devote sufficient attention to the training of observers who end up employing those instruments improperly. Accordingly, when classroom-observation evidence is going to be used in the assembly of evidence regarding a teacher's quality, a prominent concern should be the nature of the training supplied to those individuals doing the observing.

Not only should the way that this training was provided be considered, but also its *effectiveness.* And what this means is that evidence should be at hand that when a group of trained observers employ a given observation instrument to collect evidence about teachers, there is sufficient evidence about both the *accuracy* with which those observers determine what's taking place in a classroom, and also the *consistency* with which they do so. To gauge observers' consistency, levels of *inter-observer agreement* are typically calculated based on the results of different observers who have independently viewed the same classroom activities.

What we are hoping for, of course, is that when different observers watch the same actions of a teacher and the teacher's students, those observers will end up recording essentially the same events. Moreover, we'd also like some evidence, if inter-observer agreement is present, that those in-accord observers actually "got it right." That is, we want evidence that if several observers agreed a teacher was using a particular instructional technique and, therefore, satisfactory inter-observer agreement is present, then it was also the case that the particular instructional technique had, in fact, been used.

Thus, if we are to place great confidence in the evaluative evidence garnered by classroom observers, we should see that those observers have been trained effectively so there is both inter-observer agreement as well as observational accuracy present. Absent such information about observers' accuracy and agreement, caution in reliance on classroom-observation evidence is warranted.

TWO WIDELY USED OBSERVATION PROCEDURES

We now turn to brief descriptions of America's two most widely used classroom-observation systems, namely, those developed by Charlotte Danielson and by Robert Marzano. Any teacher evaluator these days who wishes to use classroom observations in a teacher-evaluation process, yet who is not conversant with at least one of these two observation systems, needs to do some serious catching up! Fortunately, whatever catching up might be required can be readily achieved by consulting the clearly written explanations of their work provided by Danielson (2007, 2011) or Marzano and his colleagues (Marzano, Frontier, & Livingston, 2011).

What you are about to read regarding these two observational approaches will be far from a thoroughgoing description of either of the two strategies. Think of what's coming in the next few pages, then, only as a "first date" with the Danielson and the Marzano ways of observing what goes on in teachers' classrooms.

Danielson's Framework for Teaching

Charlotte Danielson is an educational consultant and presenter who, based in Princeton, New Jersey, heads the Danielson Group. Her organization offers assistance to schools, districts, and states focused chiefly on the evaluation and supervision of teaching. In 1996, ASCD published the first edition of *Enhancing Professional Practice: A Framework for Teaching* (Danielson, 1996) in which Danielson provided readers with a sophisticated way of addressing the full complexity of classroom teaching. Her model became so widely used that, as Marzano and his colleagues aptly put it, "Given its past and current popularity, the Danielson model must be the reference point for any new proposals regarding supervision and evaluation" (Marzano et al., 2011, p. 23). In 2007, ASCD published a second edition of her 1996 book. The 2007 version of Danielson's framework featured several modest changes, but it did not depart in any dramatic manner from its initial structure.

Danielson's framework was based on her earlier work at the Educational Testing Service (ETS) where she and her colleagues attempted to identify research-based instructional strategies or teacher actions that, when employed by teachers, increased the likelihood of students' learning. These principles, then, were incorporated in ETS-developed licensure tests for teachers. Danielson drew heavily on these research findings when she generated her 1996 framework and its subsequent renditions.

Three levels of descriptors. In a nutshell, here's what the Danielson model is. At the most general level, it starts off with four *domains.* Domain 1 is "Planning and Preparation"; Domain 2 is "The Classroom Environment"; Domain 3 is "Instruction"; and Domain 4 deals with "Professional Responsibilities." Then, in each of these domains there are a number of more specific *components* such as, for example, in the Instruction Domain (Domain 3), Component 3a is "Communicating with Students" and Component 3c is "Engaging Students in Learning." In all, 22 components are divided almost equally among the four domains.

At an even more specific level, each component is then further divided into *elements.* All together, there are 72 elements in the 2007 Danielson framework. The elements per component range from a low of 2 to a high of 5. To illustrate, if we were to begin in the framework's Domain 2 (The Classroom Environment) and scamper down to Component 2d ("Managing Student Behavior"), we'd see there are three elements in that component, namely, "Expectations," "Monitoring of Student Behavior," and "Response to Student Misbehavior." To review, then, the Danielson Model is a three-tier descriptive system in which 72 elements are subsumed under 22 more general components that are, in turn, subsumed under four more general domains.

Four quality levels. Danielson provides rubrics that can be used when evaluating a teacher's quality according to each of the 72 elements. She employs four commonly used quality descriptors, that is, *Distinguished, Proficient, Basic,* and *Unsatisfactory.* Clearly, because each of the 72 elements deals with different aspects of the instructional process, these rubrics vary from element to element. Yet, to supply an example of what's presented in each rubric, we can look at Domain 3 (Instruction) and its Component 3d (Using Assessment in Instruction) where we find the element of "Feedback to Students." To earn a *Distinguished* designation for this element, its rubric indicates that "Teacher's feedback to students is timely and of consistently high quality, and students make use of the feedback in their learning." At the other end of the quality continuum for this particular element, an *Unsatisfactory* is to be given when "Teacher's feedback to students is of poor quality and not provided in a timely manner." Descriptions of what's needed to be assigned a *Basic* or *Proficient* level are also provided in the rubric. Notice that these element-focused rubrics can describe not only what teachers are doing, but also what students are doing.

Observable in the classroom? We see, then, that for the 2007 version of her framework, Danielson has provided educators with a 72-element evaluation system permitting a four-level quality judgment to be made for each of those elements. It should be pointed out, however, that certain of the elements deal with events not observable during a classroom visit. For instance, we see in Domain 4 (Professional Responsibilities) that several components and elements would definitely not be seen by a classroom observer. To illustrate, Component 4e (Growing and Developing Professionally) contains three elements such as "Service to the Profession" that even a properly trained, hawk-eyed classroom observer would have a tough time spotting. For teacher evaluators employing the Danielson framework, or using a derivative version of it, a decision must be made about the degree to which observation-based evidence should be restricted to domains, components, or elements actually observable during classroom visitations.

The 2011 version. In 2009, researchers sponsored by the Bill and Melinda Gates Foundation initiated a major research project (Measures of Effective Teaching) calling for the use of several observation protocols in the analysis of more than 23,000 video-captured classroom lessons. Not surprisingly, one of those observation systems was the widely used Danielson model. During this research application of the framework, several modifications were made to better carry out the training and certification of hundreds of video-lesson observers (Danielson, 2011). The essential nature of the framework was unaltered, that is, its four domains, 22 components, and 72 elements remained intact. However, the language of its rubrics was not only tightened, but those four-category rubrics were now to be applied to the framework's more general *components* rather than to its *elements*. Moreover, possible examples of performance levels were supplied for each component, as were "critical attributes" providing guidance for observers when distinguishing between practices at adjacent performance levels.

To illustrate the nature of these more general rubrics, we can consider the language employed to guide observers when assigning an *Unsatisfactory* designation for a teacher on Component 3d (Using Assessment in Instruction): "There is little or no assessment or monitoring of student learning; feedback is absent or of poor quality. Students do not appear to be aware of the assessment criteria and do not engage in self-assessment." We can see, then, that the 2011 framework represents an effort to amalgamate the existing quality distinctions among each component's elements into more comprehensive, multi-element component-based descriptions of quality. As a consequence, 22 component-focused rubrics, each of them distinguishing among *Unsatisfactory, Basic, Proficient,* and *Distinguished,* are now available for use by classroom observers employing the 2011 version of the Danielson framework.

Cautions. Danielson, perhaps because she has taught at all levels from kindergarten through college, provides practical, readily understandable descriptions of how her approach can work in the classroom. The lucidity of her explanations, without doubt, accounts at least in part for the remarkable popularity of her approach. As she candidly points out, her framework is informed by a constructivist view of learning that fosters students' active intellectual engagement as they engage in complex learning. Although the Danielson framework does not require the use of any particular instructional procedure, educators who subscribe to a more passive conception of student learning than is represented by constructivism may find certain segments of her formulation less useful.

She also makes it clear that her framework was originally developed for multiple purposes, only one of which was for teacher evaluation. Many adopters of the Danielson model did so initially because of their belief that, when used as part of a professional development strategy, it could contribute to improved conversations among educators and improved instructional practices by teachers. Greater care must be taken, as she cautions us, when using the framework as part of the high-stakes evaluation of individual teachers.

Whether the Danielson framework is used in its 2007 version or in its 2011 incarnation, and whether it is used intact or in some modified variation, users of her approach need to be thoroughly familiar with the thinking that went into this well-known approach to supervision and evaluation. Her many books, especially those focused on the 1996, 2007, and 2011 versions of the framework for teaching (Danielson, 1996, 2007, 2011), make such familiarization eminently manageable.

The Marzano Model

By the beginning of the 21st century, Robert Marzano was generally recognized as a preeminent synthesizer and describer of research results bearing on the work of educators. For example, in 2001 we saw the first of his "that works" books when ASCD published *Classroom Instruction That Works: Research-Based Strategies for Increasing Student Achievement* (Marzano, Pickering, & Pollack, 2001). During the following decade, Marzano, sometimes collaborating with others and sometimes writing solo, provided educators with a series of research-rooted guidelines dealing with such topics as classroom management, school leadership, district leadership, grading, and classroom assessment (Marzano, 2003, 2006; Marzano, Pickering, & Marzano, 2003; Marzano & Waters, 2009; Marzano, Waters, & McNutty, 2005). The expository strategy employed in these practitioner-focused books was quite consistent. First, a synthesis of extant empirical research dealing with the book's topic (for example, classroom management) was presented, typically accompanied by commentaries regarding the strength of the research findings under review. This synthesis was followed by the identification of practices that, based on the previously reviewed research, appeared to "work," that is, seemed to increase the likelihood of teachers' or administrators' attaining the results they sought. These popular volumes contributed to the widely held view that Marzano was a scholar who knew how to distinguish between wretched and respectable research investigations, and could then transform respectable evidence into understandable guidelines for real-world educators.

A cofounder and CEO of Marzano Research Laboratory in Englewood, Colorado, in recent years Marzano has sometimes turned his attention to the evaluation of teachers. In a 2011 ASCD book, along with two coauthors, *Effective Supervision: Supporting the Art and Science of Teaching* (Marzano, Frontier, & Livingston, 2011) offers an alternative approach to the observation of classroom instruction. Although this treatment of classroom observation is chiefly designed for use formatively (as part of a supervision-based strategy) to improve a teacher's instructional skill, many of the procedures proffered by Marzano and his coauthors are ideally suited for the collection of evaluative evidence regarding a teacher's quality.

A comparison of the Marzano and Danielson procedures for getting a fix on a teacher's skill will reveal several key similarities. It is also the case that the two procedures embody a number of significant differences. Teacher evaluators, if they are on the brink of opting to collect classroom-observation evidence about a teacher's ability, will find it illuminating to contrast prominent features of these two observational approaches. Although the Danielson model is employed far more frequently throughout the United States, the Marzano approach—which he and his colleagues accurately regard as "the new kid on the block"—is receiving considerable attention. For example, in the state of Washington, school-district officials can choose from three teacher-evaluation observational approaches, two of which are the Danielson and Marzano models.

Domains, subcategories, and subcategories. The Marzano model, like the Danielson model, has four domains. Domain 1 is "Classroom Strategies and Behaviors"; Domain 2 is "Planning and Preparation"; Domain 3 is "Reflecting on Teaching"; and Domain 4 deals with "Collegiality and Professionalism." Each of these four domains has subcategories, and the three subcategories in Domain 1's Classroom Strategies and Behaviors also have their own subcategories.

When considering the lowest levels of subcategories in the system, it turns out that the Marzano system has 60 elements, which, in approximate terms, reminds us of the 72 elements in the Danielson approach. Because of the importance that Marzano and his colleagues place on *classroom* strategies and behaviors, 41 of his 60 elements wind up in Domain 1. Marzano splits Domain 1 (Classroom Strategies and Behaviors) into three subcategories: Routine Segments, Content Segments, and Segments Enacted on the Spot. A "segment" in the Marzano approach is regarded as a classroom event that has a specific purpose and a particular set of strategies and behaviors designed to accomplish that purpose. Lesson segments are sometimes also referred to as "elements."

To illustrate, under the Domain 1 subcategory of Routine Segments (those that occur in every class or take place periodically in classes) we see five elements, one of which is "Tracking Student Progress." Under the Domain 1 subcategory of Content

Segments, we encounter 18 elements dealing with such lesson segments as "Previewing New Content" and "Using Homework." In
the Domain 1 subcategory of Segments Enacted on the Spot, we
also find 18 elements.

The earlier book by Marzano, *The Art and Science of Teaching:
A Comprehensive Framework for Effective Instruction* (2007), is used
in Domain 1 (Classroom Strategies and Behaviors) as a planning
framework by presenting design questions that can be used to help
group the domain's 41 elements. For example, consider Design
Question 5, "What will I do to engage students?" taken from *The
Art and Science of Teaching* book. Because this design question falls
under the Domain 1 subcategory of "Segments Enacted on the Spot,"
we find that there are nine relevant elements listed such as "Using
Academic Games" and "Maintaining a Lively Pace." As indicated,
these design questions are used only as structuring tools in subdivid-
ing Domain 1's 41 segments. Design questions are not found in the
other three domains.

Because Domain 1's classroom strategies and behaviors are not
only regarded by Marzano and his colleagues as being most significant, but because what's listed under Domain 1 represents the
things an observer can actually see when spending time watching
what takes place in class, it is apparent that, for purposes of teacher
evaluation, the 41 elements of Domain 1 are of particular importance
when collecting classroom-observation evidence of a teacher's skill.

Levels of performance. The Marzano approach to classroom
observation features five levels of performance, not a substantial
departure from the four Danielson levels, although labeled differently.
When observers are focusing on, say, one of Domain 1's 41 elements
dealing with the teacher's "Demonstrating Intensity and Enthusiasm,"
those observers can assign to it one of the following labels and
(parenthesized) points: *Innovating* (4), *Applying* (3), *Developing*
(2), *Beginning* (1), or *Not Using* (0). This five-level scale is employed
by observers when using either of two, about-to-be-described, observation instruments supplied by Marzano et al. (2011).

A pair of observation protocols. Marzano and his colleagues
provide users with two meaningfully different ways of collecting
observational evidence regarding a teacher's instruction. First, they
offer (in Marzano et al., 2011) what they describe as a Long Form
Observational Protocol that separates teacher evidence from student evidence, and particularizes the scoring rubrics provided so

that two performance levels—Developing (2 points) and Applying (3 points)—are distinctively designed for the element being considered. The other three performance levels in each rubric, that is, the Not Using (0 points), Beginning (1 point), and Innovating (4 points), are identical irrespective of the element involved. For instance, no matter which element is under consideration, a performance level of "Innovating" along with its four points is always described using the following words: "Adapts and creates new strategies for unique student needs and situations" (Marzano et al., 2011, Appendix A).

Second, a Short Form Observational Protocol is also provided in which no distinction is made between teacher evidence and student evidence, but there is a clear emphasis on observing the *teacher's* behavior and strategies. Again, the same five levels of performance are used, but not described or particularized in any way for different elements.

Because, in their 2011 *Effective Supervision* book, the Long Form Observational Protocol consumes 41 pages while the Short Form Observational Protocol only takes up 4-1/2 pages, it seems clear that Marzano and his coauthors definitely knew the difference between short and long. Teacher evaluators who are considering either of these observational protocols in relation to their own work will, of course, wish to spend time with the two meaningfully different ways of collecting observation-based evidence of a teacher's ability.

What's most crucial in the collection of classroom-observation evidence, of course, are the dimensions on which teachers are to be observed. Happily, as was true with the Danielson model, the attributes of Marzano's approach are well supported by empirical evidence—chiefly because of his conversance with empirical investigations related to education. Both the Marzano and Danielson approaches to the collection of classroom-observation evidence are surely grounded on research rather than on raw speculation.

Nearing the end of this "first date" with the Danielson and Marzano approaches to classroom observation, both strategies contain three increasingly more specific descriptive levels. The most specific aspects of Danielson's framework are distributed rather evenly among her system's four domains. Marzano's approach emphasizes the Classroom Strategies and Behaviors Domain where 41 of his 60 elements are found. Although the Danielson system relies on the use of four performance levels, the Marzano procedures use five performance levels. Closer analysis of the rubrics and scales provided for these systems, however, indicate substantial differences in how observers are to employ these performance scales.

A frequently voiced concern on the part of those educators who have employed either of these two systems is that there are simply too many factors to keep track of when evaluating teachers. In the Danielson approach, an attempt was made to provide more generic rubrics when she recently moved from 72 element-focused rubrics to 22 component-focused rubrics. However, because the distinguishing features in the reduced number of rubrics are, in fact, the 72 elements, then teacher evaluators clearly must still attend to many factors. Similarly, although Marzano emphasizes chiefly what goes on instructionally, there are still 41 elements featured in that domain. A number of users of either of these two systems, therefore, have simply reduced the number of evaluative factors involved by choosing smaller numbers of what they regard as the highest-priority ingredients in successful teaching.

Formative and summative applications. Even a superficial reading of the material explaining the derivations and applications of these two observation methods will reveal that when Danielson and Marzano developed their conceptualizations of what goes on during instruction, they were both drawn to the importance of *enhancing* a teacher's instructional skills. Neither of these observation approaches was crafted with the exclusive purpose of evaluating teachers in a summative manner. These two systems were generated, then, with the laudable intention of improving teachers' instructional prowess.

However, when either of these systems is chosen either "as is" or after having been modified, teacher evaluators need to be alert to the possibility that the formative, improvement-oriented virtues of any observational strategy must not diminish the summative, evaluation-focused dividends of the strategy. There is, clearly, a powerful need to help teachers get better at teaching. And, in order to do so, classroom observations can play a pivotal role in accomplishing that improvement-focused goal. But formative classroom observations can be carried out at different times and with different observers than when we collect summatively focused classroom-observation data. Scripture tells us that the simultaneous serving of two masters is impossible. The same is true for those who would use classroom observations at the same time to accomplish a formative as well as summative outcome. It simply can't be done.

EVIDENTIAL-WEIGHT GUIDELINES

When deciding what sorts of evidence ought to be used in the evaluation of teachers, it is definitely difficult to overlook the potential contributions of classroom observations. On political and public-relations grounds—not to mention fundamental fairness—it is probable that any sort of credible teacher-evaluation system will include at least some amount of evidence collected via classroom observations. And, if this is the case, then the following evidential-weight guidelines may be of some use in deciding how much evaluative influence should be assigned to such evidence.

- Greater evidential weight should be given to classroom-observation evidence based on extensive rather than skimpy observations of teachers in action.
- Greater evidential weight should be attributed to classroom-observation evidence derivative from instructional activities regarded as typical rather than atypical, thereby dictating the need for unannounced rather than announced observations.
- Greater evidential weight should be assigned to classroom-observation evidence collected via a proven, research-based observation instrument rather than an untried observation form whose dimensions are unsupported empirically.
- Greater evidential weight should be given to classroom-observation evidence when the observers have been sufficiently well trained so that documented accuracy of observations and inter-observer agreement of observers are present.

CHAPTER IMPLICATIONS FOR THREE AUDIENCES

For Policymakers: It is difficult to conceive of serious-minded teacher evaluation that does not contain at least some degree of classroom observation. As a consequence, educational policymakers can reasonably conclude that a segment of their state's teacher-evaluation strategy will feature classroom observations. Hopefully, the treatment of such observation-based evidence in this chapter will induce warranted caution about the variable quality of classroom-observation evaluative data. Policymakers dare not invest too much confidence in the accuracy of observation-based evidence in light of the many ways in which its value can be compromised. In particular, educational policymakers should realize that the two most widely employed classroom-observation systems now used in the United States were originally devised with a formatively focused, instructional-improvement function in mind. Care must be taken to assure that, when used for summative teacher evaluations, these systems—or state/local modifications of them—provide persuasive evaluative evidence.

For Administrators: Because district and school-site administrators are likely to be actively involved in any version of classroom observations used for teacher evaluation, it is clear that those administrators need to familiarize themselves with state-adopted observation procedures. Some states will allow districts to select from two or more state-approved observation procedures. Other states will allow substantially more—or less—latitude to local school systems. Regardless of which observational protocol(s) may have been chosen for use in a particular setting, attention should be given to the evidential-weight guidelines set forth at the chapter's conclusion. Put simply, as the chapter suggests, some observation systems are better than others, and some observation systems are better implemented than others. Finally, administrators should have no illusions about the ability of observation systems to permit fine-grained distinctions among the substantial middle-quality group of teachers in our schools.

For Teachers: Because they are the objects of classroom observations, it seems obvious that teachers themselves should be intimately familiar with whatever system is being used to collect evidence regarding their instructional quality—and dare not assume that the observation system being employed is appropriate. Realistically, if full-blown Danielson or Marzano observation models are employed in a state, then many teachers will understandably complain that too many evaluative dimensions will simply overwhelm the state's teachers. Yet, if reductions in those multidimensional models are made, are the state-chosen evaluative dimensions defensible? Also, if teachers understand the difference between formatively focused observation visits and observations intended to determine a teacher's typical instruction, then perhaps they can lobby more effectively for the much-needed separation between formative and summative teacher evaluation—a separation accompanied by observational approaches best suited for each of those two strategies.

CHAPTER 7

Evidence From Ratings

Principals have been rating teachers ever since principals first walked the earth. Indeed, principals have rated teachers for so many years that "teacher rating" has become a nearly universal job requirement for today's principals. In some settings, of course, particularly in large schools, a principal is able to hand off those teacher-rating responsibilities to another school-site administrator such as an assistant principal or a department chair. But in almost all small and mid-size schools, when someone becomes a principal, that someone is destined to supply ratings for the school's teachers.

Interestingly, while a school's principal is rating the school's teachers, those same teachers are typically being rated by numerous other people—little people. That's right; teachers are often routinely rated by many of the students they currently teach. But when students rate a teacher, they typically do so informally, and almost never see those judgments entered onto any official rating form. Yes, although not officially solicited, many students engage in a fair amount of covert and casual teacher rating as they proceed through their school years.

For children in elementary schools, students' informal ratings usually compare the quality of a current teacher to the quality of earlier teachers. Such comparisons occur, for example, when a fifth grader exclaims to a friend that "Miss Garrison, my teacher this year, is way better than my fourth-grade teacher last year." In secondary schools, we often find students comparing their current teachers to one another. For instance, we might overhear a student say, "My English teacher is definitely the worst of all the teachers I have this year. My English class gets more boring every week!"

So, because principals *must* rate teachers' quality, and because students *can* rate teachers' quality, in this chapter we will be considering another potential source of evidence by which teachers can be evaluated, namely, *ratings of a teacher's quality.* We'll deal with ratings of a teacher's quality supplied by school-site administrators as well as ratings of a teacher's quality supplied by students. Before dipping into those two kinds of ratings, however, let's briefly consider the nature of ratings themselves or, more specifically, the nature of ratings that are focused on a teacher's quality.

ROOTING AROUND WITH RATINGS

In the previous chapter, as we were looking at evidence of a teacher's quality based on classroom observations, a distinction was drawn between classroom observations and ratings. It was pointed out that, unlike the *systematic* collection of classroom-observation evidence whereby a trained observer uses a carefully developed observation form to record key events going on during a classroom session, ratings often arise less systematically. In many instances, ratings of a teacher's quality flow from a rater's reliance on less carefully structured and often diverse data. Here's my dictionary's fairly conventional definition of a rating: *A classification or ranking of someone or something based on a comparative assessment of their quality, standard, or performance* (The New Oxford American Dictionary, 2001).

Typically, when teachers are to be rated, those who do the rating are asked to supply a quality judgment about a particular teacher. That judgment is always focused on one or more things. These "things" being rated can be given many labels such as attributes, factors, dimensions, or some synonymous label. In this chapter, what's to be rated will usually be described as a *dimension,* that is, a dimension of a teacher's ability for which a quality judgment is being sought—either from students or from a school-site administrator.

Because our continuing illustration in the book deals with a teacher's *instructional ability,* a choice immediately presents itself to any teacher evaluator wishing to use ratings as part of a teacher-appraisal program. That choice hinges on whether to seek a single *one-dimensional* rating or, instead, to solicit a series of *multidimensional* ratings. A one-dimensional procedure might ask raters to supply a single, overall rating of a teacher's "instructional ability." A multidimensional approach would typically focus on what are regarded as separable dimensions of the teacher's instructional skill. When those separate ratings are subsequently coalesced, the resulting composite rating would be considered a suitable representation of a teacher's "instructional ability." Examples of the dimensions that might be included in a multidimensional approach would be a teacher's (1) clarity of explanations, (2) engagement of students in the learning process, (3) provision of suitable models for students' emulation, (4) classroom management, and so on. The actual dimensions to be chosen, of course, would depend on the conceptualizations of learning and of instruction possessed by the developers of whatever rating procedures are going to be used.

The ratings themselves are often made in the form of descriptive classifications, that is, when raters must choose among labels representing gradations of "good" or "bad." For example, raters might be asked to pin one of the following labels on a teacher for each dimension to be rated: *Excellent, Good, Acceptable, Weak,* or *Deficient.* Whatever the nature of the quality-signifying labels happen to be, they definitely need to be described well enough so that different raters can bring relatively similar interpretations to their rating tasks.

A second way that raters can designate how well a teacher stacks up on a specified dimension is to employ numerical rating scales ranging from, for instance, a "most positive" rating of 10 to a "least positive" rating of 1. Smaller point-ranges, of course, can also be employed. Many seasoned researchers who work with teacher ratings believe that most raters are simply unable to arrive at the subtle quality-distinctions necessary when one must use a many-points rating form. Thus, many researchers advocate the use of rating forms with more limited score ranges based on smaller numbers of points.

To recap, ratings of teachers are typically focused either on a single dimension or on several dimensions that, having first been collected separately, are subsequently consolidated in the form of a single, comprehensive rating. These ratings are usually supplied when raters either (1) select from a set of categories representing different levels of quality or (2) use numerical scales anchored at both ends so a rater can numerically designate a teacher's goodness or badness with respect to the dimension being rated. The potential permutations of rating scales usable in the evaluation of teachers are substantial. Clearly, then, those who devise the rating forms to be employed in teacher evaluations, and those who specify the manner in which those forms are to be used, will exert great influence on the quality of any teacher-evaluation evidence gathered via ratings.

Lurking Comparisons

An important feature about ratings is their comparative emphasis. Whereas classroom observations might focus only on identifying the *frequency* with which teachers or students display certain kinds of designated behaviors, those behaviors need not *immediately* be translated into a comparative determination of a teacher's quality. Certain teacher-evaluation observation procedures simply call for an on-the-spot designation of the number of times a specified behavior has taken place during the instructional activity observed. Later on, well after a classroom observation has been completed, these frequency counts can be converted into some sort of quality designations.

For example, let's suppose that Jolene Johnson, an elementary principal for four years, has been directed by district officials to employ the following quality labels when rating the instructional ability of her school's teachers: *Excellent, Good, Marginal,* or *Weak.* When, near the close of a school year, Jordan assigns one of these quality ratings to each of her school's teachers, you can safely bet that she will be doing a substantial amount of mental "comparing and contrasting." For example, when she gives the school's new third-grade teacher, Clyde Carter, an *Excellent* rating, Jolene might arrive at Clyde's *Excellent* rating only after making at least a rough, mental comparison of Clyde's skills with the skills of the many primary teachers she has seen in action during her experiences as a teacher, as an assistant principal, and now as a principal.

When school-site administrators or students rate teachers, then, we can safely assume that a certain degree of comparative judging will be going on in their heads. And even if the raters have been directed to employ a set of designated categories and a previously developed rubric to guide the rating process, most raters still impose their own comparative estimates of quality when choosing among a rubric's classifications. Ratings, in one way or another, are always rooted in comparative determinations of quality.

Amalgam Judgments

When most of us are asked to rate another individual, we often rely on a variety of information when arriving at our rating. For instance, if someone is asked to rate a dozen friends according to who is a "truly good friend," the rater's typical response, before arriving at a per-friend rating, will be to consider various aspects of each of those friends such as their honesty, congeniality, and supportiveness. And, sometimes, the factors a person relies on when rating Friend 1 might actually be different than the factors that person employs when rating Friend 2. Ratings, especially those made in informal situations, are often rendered after a rater has considered a varied array of comparative information.

More formally, when the performance of an Olympic springboard diver is being rated, raters consider the difficulty of the attempted dive, the way the diver is lifted upward by the diving board, the diver's body control before entering the water, and the smoothness of the diver's entry into the water. In short, when judging the performance of many athletes, raters rely on a host of different dimensions when arriving at a comparative rating for the athlete. Most ratings, indeed, are multidimensional ratings. And although the number of dimensions to be involved in a rating can be constrained substantially by a rating procedure's directives, most ratings of teachers represent comparative amalgams of those factors considered important by the rater.

In this chapter, and in the book's other four chapters about potential evidence sources, we are using an ongoing illustrative example of a single evaluative criterion, namely, a teacher's *instructional ability*. Thus, we will be looking at ratings supplied by both principals and students focused only on a teacher's instructional ability.

Three Flavors of Bias

Okay, so far we've seen that, though always dependent on the rater's comparative judgments, ratings supplied by different people are often based on a variety of factors. And this is true even if those ratings are supposed to be focused on a single evaluative criterion such as a teacher's instructional ability. Yet, in addition to ratings being comparative amalgamations drawn from diverse evidence, ratings often suffer from a serious shortcoming on the part of many raters, namely, *rater bias*. That's right; just as we saw that the items on educational tests can be biased against certain subgroups of test takers, it is also true that educational raters can be biased. Raters who are biased tend to award higher-than-warranted ratings or lower-than-warranted ratings to those being rated. The consequence of such bias tendencies, of course, is to distort the accuracy of the ratings supplied and, therefore, to reduce the validity of any ratings-based inferences about those who were rated.

Decades of experience in collecting educational ratings indicate that three kinds of rater-bias mistakes will be commonly encountered— irrespective of who or what is being rated. The first of these is called a *severity error.* This describes a rater's predisposition to supply lower ratings than, had no bias been present, the rater would have given. Raters displaying a severity bias tend to regard those individuals they are rating according to a "glass-is-half-empty" perspective whereby, if rating a person who happens to be precisely on the borderline between quality categories that are adjacent, a severity biased rater will invariably lean toward the lower of the two categories.

A second sort of rater bias is the exact opposite of a severity bias, and it occurs when a rater makes a *generosity error.* Raters who display this bias are "glass-is-half-full" folks who, upon encountering a half-filled glass, will tend to see the glass as more full than empty. When a generosity-biased rater encounters a teacher who sits qualitatively smack in the middle of two adjacent categories such as "proficient" and "distinguished," this habitually generous rater will always assign the higher of the two categories to the borderline teacher.

A third category of rater bias is somewhat more intriguing. In all instances involving qualitative ratings, we encounter raters who tend to make *central-tendency errors.* These raters are inclined to assign mid-quality ratings irrespective of whether the person being rated is definitely at either the low end or the high end of a quality distribution. For example, if a to-be-rated teacher is a fabulous instructor, simply oozing instructional wizardry, a rater afflicted with central-tendency bias would end up assigning an in-the-middle rating to this superb teacher. Yet, at the opposite end of the instructional-quality yardstick, a teacher who was unquestionably wretched would also garner an in-the-middle label from a rater afflicted with central-tendency bias. Raters who make central-tendency errors tend to be "play it safe and don't offend" sorts of individuals.

It is tempting to sneer snidely at raters who misrepresent reality by making these three kinds of errors. These raters are, in most instances, unarguably wrong. Their ratings do not jibe with what's actually there. Yet, in fairness, please recognize that raters who are prone to make severity errors, generosity errors, or central-tendency errors are rarely being willfully inaccurate. This is simply how they have learned to see the world. Their ratings biases are usually fueled by a lifetime's worth of experiences, some of which have seriously compromised the accuracy of the quality ratings they are now being asked to make. For anyone who devises a teacher-evaluation system in which evidence from ratings is to be included, it would be naïve to assume that all of the participating raters will see the world in the same way. It would be far safer to assume that, in almost all collections of raters, substantial bundles of bias exist that, with training and monitoring, can usually be reduced or eliminated.

Before leaving the distortions that rater bias, if unaddressed, can have on a teacher-evaluation program, we need to identify one final threat to the accuracy of ratings regarding a teacher's skill, namely, *halo effect.* Halo effect describes a tendency on the part of raters to allow their ratings of someone to be distorted by a single, particularly noteworthy dimension of the person who's being rated. If that solo, significant dimension is a powerfully positive one, then a rater whose judgments are distorted by halo effect will tend to see other dimensions of the rated individual as positive—even though there is no evidence attesting to such positivity. The same is true, but in the other direction, so that a particularly negative dimension will, because of halo effect, splash over onto a rater's regard for what's rated other than the especially negative dimension.

ADMINISTRATORS' AND STUDENTS' RATINGS

When attempting to identify sources of evidence that might accurately shed light on the caliber of teachers, teacher evaluators invariably consider ratings supplied by principals or other school-site administrators. In recent years, however, increased attention has been given to the role of students' ratings of their own teachers. Both of these ratings will now be considered.

Administrators' Ratings

We possess literally hundreds of years of experience in asking principals and other school-site administrators to evaluate the quality of a school's teachers. And, not surprisingly, we have learned a number of important lessons about administrators' ratings of teachers' skill. One of the most important insights obtained over the years has been the difficulty of asking a principal to function *simultaneously* as a formative evaluator and summative evaluator of a school's teachers.

The fundamental reason that a school's principal cannot supply accurate ratings while serving in these two roles at the same time stems from an incompatibility of these two evaluative functions. Given the inherent incompatibility of the formative and summative evaluative roles of principals, it makes more sense to assign a principal to *one* of the two roles, getting someone else to take on the other mission.

As has been suggested earlier, principals differ not only in what they regard as the most salient factors to employ when evaluating a teacher, but also in their access to information that could contribute to their evaluations. Even if, for instance, a teacher is to be rated exclusively on the basis of the teacher's *instructional ability,* different principals typically will bring substantially different instructional perspectives to that task. What's equally important, however, is the degree to which a principal's judgment about a teacher's instructional effectiveness is fueled by reasonable information illuminating that effectiveness. How often, for example, does a principal get an opportunity to see a teacher in action, and for how many minutes? Are these classroom visits always announced in advance and, therefore, destined to represent atypical staging on the part of the observed teacher? Are there other opportunities for the principal and a teacher to engage in nonsuperficial conversations about the instructional process and, in particular, about a teacher's personal view of instruction? Does the principal ever chat with a teacher's students in order to sample their reactions to the teacher? In short, is the information base on which a principal arrives at a conclusion about a teacher's quality substantial or slender? Clearly, the greater the amount and diversity of information a principal relies on to evaluate a teacher, the greater the confidence we can ascribe to the principal's rating of a teacher's ability.

Students' Ratings

Students have first-hand access to what goes on in a classroom and, as a consequence, can provide distinctive reactions regarding a teacher's instructional endeavors. Nor should we regard students' ratings of their teachers as a toss-in afterthought by teacher evaluators attempting to round out a set of evidence regarding a teacher's quality. In a July 11, 2012, address at the Education Commission of the States' National Forum on Education Policy in Atlanta, Bill

Gates opined that the three components constituting a good teacher-evaluation system are students' test scores, classroom observations, and *students' ratings*. If his view of the importance of students' ratings is accurate, then it is apparent that students' ratings of teachers' abilities should be given considerable attention by those who formulate any teacher-evaluation system.

Just as we saw with administrators' ratings, the dimensions on which students are to rate their teachers are always crucial, and are typically chosen by the individuals who design a teacher-evaluation system. Although it might be the choice of teacher evaluators to ask students, when rating teachers, to focus on several different dimensions of a teacher's activities, for illustrative purposes, let's stick with our example of a teacher's *instructional ability*. In that instance, the rating form to be used with students, then, would include several dimensions regarded as contributory to a teacher's instructional ability.

For instance, borrowing from Danielson's teaching framework (Danielson, 2007) treated in Chapter 6, five components are set forth under the domain of "Instruction." If we wished to do so, we could build a student rating form structured around those five components, namely, (1) Communicating With Students, (2) Using Questioning and Discussion Techniques, (3) Engaging Students in Learning, (4) Using Assessment in Instruction, and (5) Demonstrating Flexibility and Responsiveness. By employing age-appropriate language dealing with each of these dimensions, teacher evaluators could ask students to supply a rating of the teacher on each of the five dimensions. Those ratings could be made either by the student's choosing from a set of quality gradations on the rating form such as "Strong" or "Weak" or by marking a numerical scale of, say, 1 to 5 points. Having supplied ratings for each of those separate dimensions, a student might also be asked to provide a final, overall rating of the teacher's instructional ability. This, of course, is the choice of those who create the rating form.

In collecting any kind of evaluative information that has the power to have a significant impact on the life of the person being rated, there are certain data-gathering "commandments" that should always be followed. To violate these procedural guidelines is to reduce the accuracy of the evaluative evidence collected. And with regard to students' ratings of teachers, there is one sacrosanct commandment that must be followed:

Students' ratings of their teacher's abilities should always be collected in such a way that those ratings are not only anonymous, but are also perceived by the students to be anonymous.

The quest for anonymity on the part of the student-raters must be relentless. Only when students truly believe their responses cannot be traced back to them will most students respond with candid judgments about the quality of their teachers. Accordingly, the only responses students should be asked to make on a rating form should be check marks or Xs. Names, obviously, are not to be given. Nor, and this is important, should additional comments of any kind be written on the form. Students believe that their handwriting can be identified by a teacher—and students are often correct in this belief. Thus, marks only, no words, should ever be written on these teacher-rating forms. And students should be told, *in advance* of their completing a rating form, why is it that anonymity-induced candor is so important.

In addition, procedures should be installed whereby students are directed to place their completed rating forms in collection boxes so that no possibility of a teacher's identifying a student's rating form is present. And, just as the explanation of anonymity-induced candor should precede students' completion of any rating forms, these ratings-collections procedures should also be clearly explained—as well as the reason underlying them—*before* students are even given their rating forms. Ideally, the ratings-collections procedures will be standardized in schools according to a district or state decree.

Many students will have had no prior experience in supplying anonymous ratings regarding their teachers' abilities. However, with (1) an appropriate orientation to the task, (2) suitable rating forms, and (3) proper anonymity-enhancing collection procedures, students' rating of their teacher's ability can supply illuminating evidence regarding, say, a teacher's instructional ability. Let's turn, then, to a brief consideration of how to prepare raters, that is, administrators or students, for their upcoming evaluative tasks.

MAKING RATINGS RIGHTEOUS

Like any evidence-collection procedure, ratings about teachers' quality are only as good as the procedures employed to collect the evidence. Students' scores on inappropriate tests, for example, usually yield invalid inferences about teachers' skills. Similarly, classroom observations that are ill-conceived or poorly implemented typically lead to equally unsound conclusions about teachers' capabilities. And if the ratings we collect about teachers are meaningfully mistaken, then they too will lead to incorrect judgments regarding teachers' skills.

How, therefore, do we enhance the accuracy and credibility of ratings regarding teachers' quality? Interestingly, whether we are dealing with administrators' ratings or students' ratings, most of our worries about quality should be focused on (1) *the rating form* used and (2) the *preparation of the raters* to use that form.

The Rating Form

Rating forms don't float down to us from the sky—except during tornadoes. People create rating forms and, as we well know, people can mess up almost anything to which they put their minds. Because a poorly constructed rating form is practically certain to produce inaccurate judgments about a teacher's quality, it is obvious that considerable care should be devoted to the building and bettering of such rating forms. That's right, once a rating form has been constructed, it frequently requires many improvement-focused revisions until it does its rating job satisfactorily. When building a rating form from scratch, teacher evaluators rarely get it right the first time. But, of course, rating forms are rarely built from scratch. It is far more common these days for those in need of a rating form to borrow an existing form that they can use "as is" or with minor modifications. It is preferable for teacher evaluators to use an excellent rating form that's been obtained from others rather than generate an original but lower-quality rating form.

The dimensions chosen for a rating form are its most important features, and that's true with the rating forms used by both administrators or by students. Clearly, whatever those dimensions are, they should definitely have a strong bearing on a teacher's competence. Therefore, as we saw in the case of the instruments used during classroom observations, the dimensions chosen for a rating form should be based on a solid collection of empirical research showing that, for example, if a teacher engages heavily in Behavior X during class, then the teacher's students tend to learn better than the students of teachers who constantly dodge Behavior X. The stronger the research base underlying the selection of a rating form's dimensions, the more confidence we can have in the evaluative worth of judgments collected by using that rating form.

Obviously, the rating form's dimensions should be described in language clearly comprehensible to the individuals who are doing the rating. In the case of students' ratings, this means that age-appropriate language must be used to describe the rating form's dimensions. So, while a rating form for third graders and a rating form for ninth graders might both focus on identical dimensions, the verbal descriptions of those dimensions are likely to vary substantially. Similarly, the rating scale to be used by raters, whether it uses numbers or labels to represent quality gradations, should obviously be readily understandable to raters. The inclusion of examples to help guide raters is particularly helpful.

Finally, whether the rating forms chosen for a teacher-evaluation program are taken intact from another setting, or are generated anew, evidence should be at hand indicating that any rating form to be used in the high-stakes appraisal of teachers has been put through plenty of tryouts and, if necessary, revisions. For example, evidence should be available attesting to different raters' identical interpretations of the dimensions on which they are to supply ratings. Similarly, it should be demonstrated that, insofar as is reasonable, different raters tend to apply the rating form's scale in the same manner.

Put simply, because the quality of evidence collected by ratings is so dependent on the merits of the rating forms used, it should be apparent that great care must been taken to make any teacher-evaluation rating forms used as commendable as they can be.

Rater Preparation

An excellent rating form, if used *improperly,* will lead to ratings that are no better than the ratings obtained had a rancid rating form been used *properly.* In other words, ratings about a teacher's quality are dependent not only on the caliber of the rating form that's being employed, but also on the way the form is actually used. To increase the likelihood that rating forms will be used properly, and to get raters ready to rate teachers accurately, we must *prepare* those raters for their evaluative tasks.

Most school-site administrators, of course, are well versed in the use of rating forms to judge their school's teachers. That's because they have been providing such ratings since first becoming school-site administrators. The preparation given to those sorts of administrators, in advance of their actual rating of teachers, can sometimes be rather perfunctory. If an administrator has acquired any sort of serious error tendencies such as a disposition to make severity errors, then some sort of "remedial" rater guidance will be necessary. What's most needed is reasonable certainty that a prospective rater is clearheaded about what the requested ratings really mean. If the descriptive "how-to-use" material accompanying an *administrative* rating form spells out the nature of the evaluative dimensions involved, and the way the form's response scale is to be used, then little more than the provision of such explanatory materials is typically needed. With *students,* however, the preparation ground rules are quite different.

Few students have ever supplied formal, "these really count" evaluative ratings of their teachers. Those students who have done so were typically responding to some kind of teacher-made rating form that was designed chiefly to help the teacher improve. That is, the sorts of students' rating forms used in the recent decades have typically been collected as part of teachers' *formative* attempts to improve their instruction. But the kind of teacher evaluation being treated in this book is exclusively of a *summative* nature. And, although the recent flurry of state teacher-evaluation programs may ultimately see millions of students evaluating their teachers, it will be wiser during the next decade or so to assume that students know little about how to rate their teachers. Accordingly, we need to *prepare* students to supply teacher ratings that will be sufficiently accurate.

The specific nature of the preparation we supply to students who will be asked to rate their teachers should surely vary according to the ages of the students involved and any previous experience they have had in the teacher-rating process. The more mature the student, the more likely it is that the student can readily grasp how to complete a rating form that, along with the ratings of other students, will provide useful evidence about a teacher's skill. The younger the students, the more simple will be the language that should be employed when describing to students the following:

- *Why the ratings are being sought.* It is important for students to understand what use will be made of their ratings. Insofar as the ratings will be employed in a summative manner, it may be sufficient to employ age-appropriate language explaining that "Your ratings, and those of the other students in your class, will be used—along with other information—to help evaluate your teacher." If the ratings were focused on a single dimension such as, for example, a teacher's instructional ability, then students should be told that the purpose of the ratings is to help determine (or judge, evaluate, appraise) "your teacher's instructional ability." Language describing the educational importance of this activity should be included.

If it can be said to students, in honesty, that teachers will be supported in dealing with any identified instructional weaknesses, this point should definitely be made. Students who recognize that their teachers will have an opportunity to address any instructional deficits will usually be more honest when rating their teachers.

- *What the rating form's evaluative dimensions mean.* Although the rating form itself is likely to contain at least abbreviated descriptions of the rating form's dimensions, it is often helpful to amplify those descriptions, in writing or orally, so that the students have a better idea about the dimensions on which they are supplying ratings. In general, fewer evaluative dimensions will lead to more careful ratings by students than will numerous evaluative dimensions. Too many dimensions tend to foster hurried, often superficial ratings, especially by those students who are eager to wrap up the rating task.

- *How the rating form's response options are to be used by raters.* The rating form's response scale, whether it consists of descriptive categories or numbers, ought to be explained. The need for students' thoughtful use of the response scale should be stressed. As with the number of dimensions to be rated, a modest number of quality gradations will usually be preferable to the use of so many qualitative distinctions that student raters will be unable to make the sometimes subtle differentiations being asked of them.

- *The importance of honesty and its relationship to anonymity.* Even though an earlier effort should have been made to describe the function of the ratings being sought, and the importance of that function, it is nonetheless necessary to stress the need for honest ratings of a student's teacher. In that connection, a reiteration of the need for only anonymous responses should be supplied—along with a description of the identity-protecting procedure devised for students to first make their ratings and, thereafter, to submit their completed ratings.

In a manner that is age appropriate for the students involved, the above information should be made available to the students who are being asked to supply ratings of their teachers. In addition, if possible, illustrations (and explanations) of how a teacher might be rated on each dimension of the rating form could be supplied.

The Old and the New

Wrapping up, then, what about ratings as a source of evidence by which to evaluate teachers? Should teacher evaluators incorporate ratings of teachers' quality in their teacher-appraisal programs? As with each of the kinds of evidence being considered in these five chapters, this is precisely the question facing those who wish to devise a defensible teacher-evaluation program. Should evidence from ratings be used in teacher evaluation and, if so, how much weight should be given to such evidence?

Well, in the case of ratings, it surely depends on who it is that supplies the ratings. In the chapter, we have explored ratings supplied by school-site administrators and ratings supplied by students. Substantial differences between those two sorts of evidence certainly exist. We have had many, many years' worth of experience with administrators' ratings. In most instances, experienced educators know the strengths and weaknesses of such ratings. One of the nontrivial problems facing teacher evaluators who would embrace administrator ratings is how to disentangle the formative, improvement-focused function of such ratings from the summative, high-stakes evaluation function of such ratings. School principals have wrestled with this improvement-versus-appraisal dilemma for decades. On the other hand, the use of students' ratings of teachers' abilities—particularly as part of a high-stakes evaluation of teachers—is a relatively "new game in town." Frankly, we know much less about how to make students' ratings of their teachers a useful contributor to the evaluation of teachers.

As we think about the differences between students' and administrators' ratings, it once more becomes apparent how the evaluative significance of different evidence sources can vary. For openers, not only is there a fundamental difference between administrative ratings of teachers and ratings of those same teachers by their students, but there can also be substantial differences in the quality of the evidence collected via either procedure. For instance, how much evaluative weight should be given to a principal's ratings of a teacher's effectiveness when the principal's rating is based on a loose, half-hearted effort to get a fix on each teacher's true skills? Conversely, how much evaluative weight should be given to a principal's rating if the principal has implemented a careful evaluative approach involving reasonable inputs drawn from classroom visitations, instruction-related conversations with teachers, and learning-focused interviews with students? Clearly, the quality of the evidence-gathering process should determine not only *whether* administrative ratings should be included in a teacher-evaluation program, but also how much weight to give such ratings if they are included.

Similarly, if students' ratings of their teacher's competence are collected in a slapdash fashion with little preparation of students—and under conditions of debatable anonymity—the resulting ratings should surely be given little weight. On the contrary, if student ratings are collected with consummate care—carefully attending to rater-preparation and anonymity considerations—then not only might teacher evaluators be inclined to include such evidence in their evaluative procedures, but this evidence could be given substantial weight in the way a teacher is ultimately evaluated.

With ratings' evidence, as is true with all other evidence that might be employed to evaluate a teacher, the manner in which the evidence is collected should help teacher evaluators decide whether to use the evidence at all and, if so, how much weight to give it. There is no teacher-evaluation evidence that can't be corrupted. The challenge for teacher evaluators is to make the evidence selected to evaluate teachers provide optimally accurate estimates of a teacher's competence.

EVIDENTIAL-WEIGHT GUIDELINES

As might be inferred from what's been treated thus far in the chapter, decisions about whether to use ratings' evidence in a teacher-evaluation process hinge heavily on the caliber of the rating procedures employed. Given the nature of the specifics in an administrator-based rating operation, or a student-supplied ratings operation, we might easily vote an emphatic *Yes* on one rating source and an equally assertive *No* on the other. Or, of course, we could choose to use both administrative ratings and student ratings, making sure that both ratings were as sound as they could be.

- Greater evidential weight should be given to administrators' summative ratings of teachers' skill when the rating form used has been shown to be suitable, efforts have been made to orient raters, and the ratings are based on a range of quality-relevant information.
- Greater evidential weight should be given to students' ratings of a teacher's skill when the rating form used has been shown to be suitable, students have been carefully prepared for their rating tasks, and both actual and perceived rater anonymity are present.

CHAPTER IMPLICATIONS FOR THREE AUDIENCES

For Policymakers: If educational policymakers are located in a state where, in response to federal initiatives, a "multiple-measures" teacher-evaluation system has been adopted, then two particularly appealing types of evaluative evidence will be administrative ratings and students' ratings of teachers' abilities. However, as the chapter emphasizes, the quality of evidence yielded by such ratings will depend heavily on the nature of the rating forms employed and the preparation of the raters for their evaluative tasks. Policymakers, then, just as they dare not assume "a test is a test is a test," should never assume that "a rating is a rating is a rating." Educational policymakers should demand the installation of high-quality rating procedures from both administrators and students, then make sure those ratings are, indeed, defensible.

For Administrators: Although educational administrators will, naturally enough, be inclined to center their attention on the evaluative ratings they will be asked to supply themselves, those administrators also need to become familiar with the way to make student ratings more than a "popularity contest" or an "opportunity for payback" against task-master teachers. Both student and administrative ratings can contribute to the accurate appraisal of a teacher—if well conceived and skillfully collected. Administrators, therefore, need to dig into the viscera of both types of ratings. And, as usual, administrators must be attentive to the crucial distinction between whether ratings of teachers are supplied for formative or summative purposes.

For Teachers: Teachers should not assume, automatically, that the rating forms and rating-preparation procedures being used to appraise them are well founded. It would be a mistake for teachers to meekly accept the quality of administrative or student ratings— the forms themselves or the preparation of the raters. Consequently, teachers need to become familiar with the specifics of the rating procedures being used so they can raise concerns if it appears a less than suitable rating form or collection process is being employed.

CHAPTER 8

Evidence From Sundry Sources

This chapter deals with possible teacher-evaluation evidence other than the evidence sources we've considered thus far. We'll be looking in the chapter at almost a dozen potential sorts of evidence, many of which have found their way into past or present teacher-evaluation programs. The chapter's mission, then, is to bring to your attention these evidence options because one or more of them might be regarded by teacher evaluators as sufficiently worthwhile to be incorporated in a teacher-evaluation program.

The chapter is entitled *Evidence From Sundry Sources*. Of those four words, surely the least frequently used is *Sundry*. The dictionary defines *sundry* as being "several" or "of various kinds." Accordingly, the current chapter could have just as easily been entitled *Evidence From Several Sources*. However, the choice of *sundry* rather than *several* was intended to add an aura of class to a chapter that, otherwise, might have been disdained as a collection of miscellaneous evidence options. *Sundry* will, surely, increase the seriousness with which you read this chapter. Or not.

What you will encounter in the chapter is quite straightforward. In an alphabetized sequence (to avoid any perceived authorial advocacy), a set of 11 potential evidence sources will be identified. Each will be briefly described and, when warranted, their advantages and disadvantages identified. If any of these sources were to be included in a teacher-appraisal program, it is apparent that the evidential weight to be assigned to this kind of evidence would depend not only on the evidence source's power to illuminate a teacher's quality, but also on the adequacy with which the specific evidence gathering was carried out.

ALTERNATIVE SOURCES OF EVIDENCE FOR EVALUATING TEACHERS

Let us turn, now, to a series of possible evidence options that might help us evaluate the competence of a teacher. Teacher evaluators would determine whether any of these options should be regarded as (1) a significant source of evaluative evidence, (2) only a supplemental form of less important evidence, or (3) an altogether inappropriate source of evidence for appraising teachers. Here, then, are 11 potential sources of evaluative evidence that might be considered by teacher evaluators.

Academic Achievements

In a perfect world, we would pay workers what they are worth. This premise surely applies to teachers as well as to other workers. Thus, in settings where teachers have historically been paid higher salaries once they've earned advanced degrees, the rationale for such salary schedules is that teachers with stronger academic achievements will perform better than will teachers with weaker academic achievements. There is, unfortunately, meager evidence to support this rationale.

Indeed, in some school districts it has been a common salary stance to boost teachers' annual recompense if teachers have earned a master's degree *of any sort,* not necessarily a degree focally related to what those teachers are teaching. Accordingly, if a social studies teacher whose class assignments consist exclusively of teaching courses in history or geography had earned a master's degree in, say, animal husbandry, then this social studies teacher would receive a substantial salary boost.

More recently, in those school districts where more degrees entitle teachers to higher salaries, it is often insisted that only specified master's degrees—degrees germane to what a teacher is officially certified to teach—will lead to salary increases. Similar constraints are often included these days for teachers who have earned doctoral degrees. That is, to garner maximum salary increases (or, in some districts, to secure *any* salary increases), an earned doctorate must be demonstrably related to a teacher's instructional responsibilities.

The problem now facing many school-district officials is how to treat those degrees awarded by one of today's rapidly multiplying online universities. In the past, almost all advanced degrees were only offered by established colleges and universities—institutions that had been thoroughly accredited by respected accreditation groups. Now, however, we see a galaxy of independent institutions offering online degrees tailored to the needs of "busy educators." Some of these degree programs, offered online or on campus, are surely worthwhile. Some are not. Given the plethora of these recently established institutions of higher learning, not to mention the diversity of their quality, a nontrivial challenge for school-district officials is to determine which teachers actually warrant salary increases and which teachers don't.

Most fundamentally, the question before any thoughtful creator of a teacher-evaluation program is whether, when appraising two teachers working in the same setting, if all other evidence of teaching quality is precisely equal, is the teacher with additional advanced degrees more skilled than the teacher without those advanced degrees? Because teacher evaluation these days has implications not only for a teacher's salary, but also for a teacher's continued employment, the absence of definitive empirical evidence showing that additional academic accomplishments are related to teachers' instructional effectiveness should disincline most teacher evaluators to include this sort of evaluative evidence in their teacher-appraisal strategies.

Changes in Students' Affect

Students' *affect* refers to students' attitudes, interests, and values. Despite today's overriding focus on enhancing students' cognitive skills and knowledge, many educators regard students' affect as substantially more important than students' cognitive accomplishments. To illustrate, if an English teacher can engender more positive attitudes toward learning per se on the part of her students, then those students will be more likely to become lifelong learners even if they never understand the subtle distinctions she had drawn between gerunds and participles. Similarly, if a mathematics instructor is able to get his students to master all sorts of advanced mathematics operations, but in the process also makes his students despise mathematics, then those math-moxie students will rarely employ their mathematical prowess later on—when they don't have to. Yes, students' affective dispositions are important.

A potential kind of evidence regarding a teacher's effectiveness, therefore, might be pre-instruction to post-instruction shifts in students' attitudes, interests, and values. Because *values* modifications can, if teachers are not careful, stray into controversy-laden arenas best left to children's families, let's focus only on *attitudes* and *interests*. Examples of suitable attitudes to focus on when collecting this kind of evidence might be (1) students' attitudes toward the role of "effort" in the learning process, or (2) students' attitudes toward individuals from racial groups other than their own. Examples of appropriate interests to be assessed for teacher-evaluation purposes might be (1) students' interest in the subject being taught, for example, students' interest in chemistry, or (2) students' interest in reading.

But can students' affect be accurately assessed? Well, for individual students, the answer to this important assessment question is a regrettable *No.* That is, it is nearly impossible, short of invasive physiological measurements, to arrive at valid inferences about an *individual's* affective status. However, it is definitely possible to arrive at sufficiently valid inferences about a *group's* affective status— such as the affective dispositions of an entire class of students. And, because we are attempting to isolate a teacher's contribution to students' affective shifts, a group-based inference about students' attitudes and interests is really all we need. To illustrate, let's say that Mr. Johnson's fifth-grade class starts off the school year with decidedly negative attitudes toward volitional reading, that is, negative dispositions toward any on-your-own reading for pleasure. However, at the end of the school year, those same students display markedly improved, decidedly positive attitudes toward volitional reading. Shouldn't this positive evidence be incorporated when we appraise Mr. Johnson's ability?

The way we get a group-focused fix on students' affect is quite straightforward. We employ anonymously completed affective inventories in which students are presented with a small number of statements such as the following positive sentiment: "I really enjoy reading when I can choose my own books and magazines," or the following negative sentiment: "I much prefer watching television to free-time reading." Given, say, 5–10 such statements, students then respond by indicating whether (and how much) they agree or disagree with each statement, for example, on a scale ranging from "Strongly Agree" to "Strongly Disagree." Students do not give their names and are directed to make no written comments on their inventories. After the completed inventories have been collected in a manner ensuring students' anonymity (such as by having students personally deposit their own completed inventories in a designated collection box), responses for all students are scored so that the *average* affective score (usually the median, that is, the midpoint score) for the entire group of students is calculated. Typically, the higher the affective score, the more appropriate is the affect a student group is displaying.

Although the creation of these sorts of self-report affective inventories is surely not mindless, their construction and refinement represents a definitely doable task for teacher evaluators. The step-by-step procedures to generate such affective inventories are described elsewhere (Popham, 2014).

The virtue of this sort of affective evidence, collected on a pretest-posttest basis, is that it deals with an educationally significant outcome, yet can be obtained at relatively modest cost and with little intrusion on teachers' ongoing instruction. Moreover, the recognition on teachers' part that evidence regarding their affective impact on students will influence a teacher's evaluation will, in most instances, incline teachers to give instructional attention to the promotion of students' appropriate attitudes and interests.

Given that the method of obtaining students' responses is anonymous, this diminishes the tendency for students to supply "socially desirable" responses (that is, responses they believe their teachers will want). However, particularly with students who are older, some students will supply less than honest levels of agreement in response to an inventory's statements simply to "butter up" an esteemed teacher or, conversely, to "get even" with a disliked teacher. But, because many of these too-positive or too-negative responses will typically be disregarded by the selection of students' median scores, a sufficiently accurate estimate of a student group's affective dispositions can usually be secured via the use of these sorts of self-report affective inventories.

Care must be taken not to over-use affective inventories so that students become too focused on the affective dimensions being assessed. If students, perhaps in collaboration, set out to distort the accuracy of affective evidence, they usually can do so. (If used infrequently, affective assessments are less apt to spur such distortions.) When teacher evaluators employ evidence related to shifts in students' affect, those evaluators should—perhaps by chatting occasionally with a small sample of students—gauge the extent to which students seem to be responding honestly to these sorts of self-report inventories.

If properly crafted, anonymous self-report affective inventories can be employed to collect useful evidence regarding the degree to which teachers have been able to induce changes in students' affect—in either favorable or unfavorable directions. This source of evidence would seem suitable, therefore, to help evaluate a teacher's instructional ability. Clearly, the quality of the development, refinement, and administration of anonymously completed affective inventories should determine whether to employ such evidence and, if so, how much weight to attribute to any teacher-triggered shifts in students' affect.

Lesson Plans

Some researchers, over the years, have suggested that we can gain insights regarding the quality of teachers' instructional plans by examining teachers' lesson plans. Many school principals seem to agree, for teachers are often obliged to make their lesson plans available during conferences with their administrators. These conferences, when focused on the consideration of a teacher's lesson plans, are carried out most frequently as part of a more formative, improvement-focused supervisorial activity than as a summative, evaluation-focused activity.

The argument in favor of using lesson plans as evidence of a teacher's competence is that the competent teacher will include elements in lesson plans representing a superior understanding of the instructional process than will be true for a less competent teacher. In other words, skilled teachers will—on average—design activities for their students that are more consistent with research-supported ("likely payoff") instructional principles than will—on average—unskilled teachers. This is an appealing rationale for the role of lesson-plan analyses as a form of teacher-evaluation evidence. The only flaw in the argument is the "on average" part. This is because, when we evaluate teachers, we evaluate one teacher at a time. Thus, if a particular teacher does not plan to use instructional activities that—on average—work, the teacher may nonetheless get positive results with students. In Chapter 2 it was pointed out that specific teachers may carry out instruction in very different ways from what the research evidence suggests, yet still be effective teachers. And therein, of course, lies the problem with analyses of teachers' lesson plans as a serious contributor to the evaluation of teachers.

Another problem with the appraisal of teachers' lesson plans is that such analyses, at least in certain instances, may turn out to be, in the main, evaluations of a teacher's *lesson-planning skill,* not the teacher's *teaching skill.* It is surely the case that some teachers are far better devisers of instructional plans than are other teachers. What we are unable to discern, however, based *only* on lesson-plan analyses, is whether these better lesson planners are also better lesson-plan deliverers. To evaluate teachers accurately, we need to determine how well those teachers actually teach—perhaps by watching them in action or by assessing their impact on students. Skillfully planned lessons will, more often than not, lead to well taught lessons. But well taught lessons *can* take place even in the absence of well planned lessons.

And this is why it is difficult to rely on lesson-plan analyses to gauge a teacher's instructional ability. Although it is true that the scrutiny of a teacher's lesson plans can be wonderfully catalytic in a formative context where the focus of a teacher and a supervisor is on improving the teacher's instruction, for summative purposes lesson-plan analyses have scant worth.

Opportunity-to-Learn Student Surveys

One of the more important legal rulings related to public schooling were the findings of a federal court in the 1981 *Debra P. v. Turlington* case regarding the state of Florida's plan to use a basic-skills test to deny students a high school diploma. Debra P., an African American student, and several other African American students had brought a class-action suit against Ralph Turlington, Florida's Education Commissioner, to prevent him from denying diplomas to students because of their performance on a statewide achievement test. In a ruling rendered by federal judge George C. Carr, and subsequently upheld by a federal appellate court, it was decreed that a public high school diploma—because it represented a citizen's *constitutionally guaranteed* property right—could not be denied by a test covering content that students had not been taught. Because of the significance of Judge Carr's ruling, in the 30-plus years following the *Debra P.* case, educators who construct high-stakes achievement tests have been attentive to whether what is measured by their tests have, in fact, been taught to students.

Even though students in lower grades, for example, in elementary schools, are not being tested on any diploma-denial examinations, the *Debra P.* ruling still causes concern to some educators because its findings continue to function as the operative case law in much educational test-related litigation. Thus, for example, if it could be demonstrated that a particular lower-grade teacher had not provided instruction directed toward a state's officially approved (and subsequently assessed) curricular aims, a school district might conceivably be liable if disgruntled parents initiated a suit on the grounds that their child had not been given a suitable "opportunity to learn."

Because of concerns about whether teachers have been devoting adequate instructional attention to their students' mastery of official state-set curricular goals, it would be possible to collect self-report survey evidence from students regarding whether they had been given instruction related to specific curricular goals. Interestingly, this same data-gathering procedure was employed in the research study used during the *Debra P.* trial (Popham & Lindheim, 1981). In that investigation, Florida students were presented with examples of test items representing the various skills measured by the state's diploma-denial test. One skill at a time, students were not asked whether they had *mastered* the skill represented but, instead, were asked whether they had been given sufficient instruction so that they *could have mastered* the skill. The results of those opportunity-to-learn student surveys, because they provided emphatic evidence that the students had been given adequate opportunity to learn, were particularly persuasive to the *Debra P.* court.

The inclusion of evidence collected from students' responses to opportunity-to-learn surveys would be based on the argument that a competent teacher is one who provides students with the opportunities to learn what their state's educational authorities say those students are supposed to learn. Whether the students, having been provided with those opportunities, actually achieve the sought-for curricular aims, of course, is not determinable from students' responses to these opportunity-to-learn surveys. Students' performances on appropriate assessments would be needed to arrive at a conclusion about students' post-instruction levels of achievement. Yet, the use of opportunity-to-learn student surveys at least addresses the important issue of whether a teacher is dishing up the curricular content that students are officially supposed to find on their instructional plates.

If opportunity-to-learn surveys similar to those used in the *Debra P.* case were to be included in a teacher-evaluation program, it would be necessary, of course, to create suitable surveys that properly represented the key curricular targets for which a teacher is responsible. Regrettably, in most states we find that the number of curricular targets, at least those stated at the level of specificity that would make sense to students, is far too large. We really can't do a very good job in checking out opportunity to learn in a given teacher's class if that teacher is obliged to pursue so many curricular targets that students cannot be presented with suitably brief self-report surveys to complete. However, if the number of official curricular targets involved is more reasonable, for example, a dozen or less per subject, then a small cluster of illustrative items could adequately represent each curricular aim. Students could be asked something along these lines: "Please look over the sample items on this page, then indicate whether you were taught how to answer items like these."

As with all of the student self-report surveys we have considered, opportunity-to-learn surveys should be completed anonymously by students—responding only with Xs or check marks. No names or written comments should be sought, and suitably anonymous collection procedures should be employed.

When teacher evaluators contemplate the appropriateness of including an opportunity-to-learn survey in the evidence-gathering arsenal for their teacher-appraisal programs, their decision should probably depend on the degree to which they believe the most compelling evidence for determining teachers' quality has already been identified for collection. If it has, then it seems that more effort needn't be expended to make sure that additional kinds of evaluative evidence are snared. Consequently, opportunity-to-learn evidence is probably not needed. If, however, the most significant sources of evaluative evidence are *not* going to be available, then a positive decision might be made regarding inclusion of opportunity-to-learn student surveys to augment the available evaluative evidence.

Parental Engagement

Do teachers reach out to their students' parents? *Should* teachers reach out to their students' parents? Depending on the answers to those two questions, another potential source of evaluative evidence might be considered. If the architects of a teacher-evaluation system regard a teacher's parental-outreach efforts as a positive factor in judging the teacher, then consideration should be given to the inclusion of evidence related to how much effort a teacher has made to engage parents in the educational process.

Teachers can be asked to describe, probably in relatively brief terms so that this reporting activity does not become too burdensome, the specific things they did (if any) during the school year to stimulate parental engagement in promoting students' learning. In most settings, because it will be sufficiently easy for school administrators to verify the accuracy of these reports, teacher evaluators who request teachers' reports regarding their parental-engagement efforts tend to accept teachers' self-described accounts as being accurate descriptions.

If this sort of evidence is to be sought, then teachers should be given guidance regarding how to report their parental-outreach efforts. Provision of a few samples illustrating the ways teachers might describe such activities would be helpful.

Remember, whether or not to include teachers' self-described initiatives in the realm of parental engagement depends most heavily on whether the promotion of parental involvement is regarded at sufficiently worthwhile to incorporate, as a separate source of evidence, in the teacher-evaluation system being built.

Parent Ratings

Few seasoned educators dismiss the importance of parents in the educational process. If students come to a teacher's class from homes in which education is cherished, and those students have been routinely supported in school by their parents, then the teacher's instructional tasks have been made markedly more manageable. But conceding the significance of parents in the educational process is not the same thing as saying parents are able to supply informative evaluative ratings of teachers' effectiveness. And yet, another potential source of evidence sometimes considered for inclusion in a teacher-evaluation program consists of parent ratings of their children's teachers.

Let's try out the possibility of parents' ratings as a way of illuminating evaluative judgments about a teacher's *instructional ability*. If we're building a teacher-evaluation process focused on this evaluative criterion by which to judge teachers, will parent ratings of a teacher's instructional ability improve the accuracy of the evaluative judgments we make about a particular teacher's instructional ability?

This, indeed, is the crux of the choice facing teacher evaluators as they try to decide whether to incorporate any potential evidence source in a teacher-appraisal program. Putting it differently, will the inclusion of the particular evidence source under consideration actually enhance the accuracy with which teachers are evaluated? Let's face it, teacher evaluators should not be seeking a wide array of different sorts of evidence merely because a larger number of evidence sources seems more compelling than a smaller number of evidence sources. What's always being sought, therefore, as you consider this chapter's sundry sources of evidence, is the sort of information that's contributory to more accurate evaluations of teachers.

In the case of parent ratings of a teacher's instructional ability, what access do parents have to any sort of information that really bears on a teacher's instructional ability? This is the question that tends to diminish the potential value of parent ratings as a source of evaluative evidence. Rarely, if ever, do parents observe a teacher's actual teaching as it takes place. Most of parents' information about a teacher's instructional effectiveness comes from their children's accounts of what goes on in school. Occasionally, perhaps during teacher-parent conferences or similar interactions, a parent will gain some insights about the way a teacher thinks about the instructional process. But not often.

And then there is the nature of a teacher's homework assignments to students that, when considered by parents, can influence a parent's perception of the teacher's competence. Homework assignments that are definitely challenging and thought-provoking will incline parents to regard a teacher favorably; homework assignments that are patently low-level "busy work" will lead to parents' negative regard for a teacher's instructional ability.

Yet, if we were to coalesce all of a parent's likely sources of information about a teacher's skill, then weigh the evaluative influence of the resultant parent ratings, it is likely that the persuasiveness of parent ratings would be outweighed by a number of other kinds of evaluative evidence. Parent ratings molded by children's descriptions are little more than "hearsay" evidence. And those who have viewed many TV courtroom contests surely know that hearsay evidence rarely is admitted into evidence by a competent judge.

Professional Development

As is true with evidence linked to teachers' advanced degrees, we often see educators' salary schedules in which teachers can garner additional remuneration if they demonstrate that they have taken part in activities intended to improve their professional skills. As with advanced-degree evidence, such salary boosts based on increased professional development are predicated on the belief that if teachers possess more instructionally relevant knowledge and skills, those increased skills and knowledge will make teachers more instructionally effective. This is the rationale, then, for linking augmentations in a teacher's professional knowledge or skills to increases in a teacher's earnings.

Yet, while we can surely mount a meaningful argument in favor of professional-development payoffs for teachers, does this argument apply to all teachers or, instead, only to most teachers? To illustrate, ample evidence now exists to show that when teachers supply their students with descriptive and focused feedback rather than general and comparative feedback, greater learning typically takes place. In other words, if a teacher lets students know the nature of shortcomings in their efforts, and informs them about what needs to be done to improve, this feedback works far better than if a teacher only supplies very general feedback or feedback comparing students to one another. Okay, let's say that 100 teachers routinely give their students descriptive-focused feedback while 100 other teachers routinely give their students only general-comparative feedback. In that instance, would the 100 "fine feedback" teachers promote more learning for their students than would the 100 "foul feedback" teachers? In general, the answer to that question is clearly *Yes,* but this *Yes* was supplied *in general.* The implication of this distinction for the evaluation of a *particular* teacher is substantial. What it means is that particular teachers can fail to employ high-payoff instructional guidelines, yet still get good results with their students.

What's advocated in most professional development activities are teachers' adoption of "likely payoff" instructional procedures, and greater use of those instructional procedures most definitely should be encouraged by educational authorities. The more teachers who engage in research-ratified instructional activities, the better educated our children will usually be. However, and for purposes of teacher evaluation this is super-important, the evaluation of a particular teacher dare not be predicated on the teacher's use or non-use of procedures that *probably* lead to improved students' learning. Teacher evaluation is a teacher-specific enterprise, not an in-general evaluative enterprise.

Ratings by Colleagues

Another potential source of evidence intended to illuminate our judgments about a teacher's instructional ability might be based on the opinions of a teacher's colleagues. After all, many teachers in a school often form opinions about the instructional capabilities of other teachers in that school. Should we not be trying to take into consideration the opinions of these judgment-rendering teachers by incorporating some version of a collegial rating system? The ratings might be akin to those described in the previous chapter wherein administrators or students were asked to rate a teacher's instructional ability. It would be relatively simple to create a system in which teachers supplied anonymous ratings of their colleagues' teaching prowess at various points in a school year.

Two difficulties preclude our placing much reliance on teachers' ratings of their colleagues' instructional effectiveness. First, unlike ratings supplied by students who have constant awareness of their teacher's instruction, or unlike ratings supplied by administrators who can, if they wish, obtain substantial information regarding teachers' instruction, most teachers have essentially zero opportunities to see their fellow teachers in action. It is unlikely that a particular teacher will ever receive accurate ratings of their teaching skills from other teachers who have never observed that teacher's instructional efforts.

And second, even in those modest numbers of settings in which some sort of peer-observation system allow teachers to systematically visit other teachers' classrooms, there is still the difficulty of coping with the perception that "reciprocal back-scratching" will take place. Such evaluative reciprocity might occur not because of a deliberate, conspiratorial distortion, but because it is quite difficult for teachers to supply colleagues with low ratings. Understandably, it is tough for a teacher to ladle out a less than positive rating for a colleague when, perhaps for decades, they might be sharing coffee or yogurt in their school's faculty lounge.

Given these two deficiencies, that is, insufficient observation opportunities and the likelihood of teachers' supplying ratings containing too many generosity errors, teachers' ratings of their colleagues' instructional ability are rarely proffered as a serious source of evidence for evaluating teachers.

Student Interviews

If it is true that students, because of their intimate familiarity with their teachers' instruction, can provide us with anonymous ratings of their teachers' skills, isn't it also possible to garner similar insights from students by interviewing students one at a time or in small groups? The general answer to that question is an emphatic *No.* Two significant problems must be recognized with the use of evidence from student interviews as a way of evaluating teachers. Taken together, these two deficits should dissuade teacher evaluators from attempting to incorporate student-interview data as an evidence component in a teacher-evaluation program.

First, and definitely foremost, one of the genuine reasons that anonymous students' ratings of a teacher's instructional ability are so evaluatively valuable is that those ratings are *anonymous.* Operating under the cloak of anonymity, most students believe it is sufficiently safe so that they can tell the truth about their teacher's ability. With in-person student interviews, anonymity flies out the window. Accordingly, a student who—when responding anonymously to a rating form—feels safe enough to rate a teacher negatively might be too intimidated to do so during a face-to-face interview. After all, even if the interviewer might have earnestly promised not to reveal a student's responses to the interviewer's questions, many interviewees will be less than candid because of the mere possibility their negative opinion of a teacher will somehow find its way back to the teacher who is being rated. Whether involving a solo, one-student-at-a-time interview or a group interview of, say, a half-dozen students at once, live interviews preclude respondents' anonymity and, thereby, will reduce the response honesty of otherwise honest students.

A second problem with student interviews is that they take time, a great deal of time. Given what we can secure from them in the way of useful evidence, student interviews simply consume too much time—from teacher evaluators and from students themselves. If substantial numbers of student interviews are to be carried out—whether those interviewers are certificated educators or are lower-paid personnel—the costs of student interviews are usually prohibitive.

Although student interviews have scant utility as evidence contributing to the appraisal of a teacher's ability, such interviews can sometimes be employed to verify that other evaluative evidence regarding a teacher's skill has been properly obtained. For instance, suppose a teacher supplies convincing evidence that, on a teacher-made test, students have demonstrated dramatic pretest-to-posttest improvements in mastering the cognitive skills measured by the test. Interviews with small samples of the teacher's students could be used to confirm that the teacher did not give students twice as much time to complete posttests in contrast to the abbreviated pretest's time allocation. Student interviews, then, can supply confirmatory evidence about the legitimacy of other kinds of evidence such as students' attitudinal shifts. Teacher evaluators, by making certain there was neither "hanky" nor "panky" associated with such evidence, can regard such evidence with warranted confidence.

Teacher-Made Tests

To confirm that a teacher is providing instruction aligned with officially designated curricular targets, as well as to ensure that teachers are aiming their classroom instruction at sufficiently lofty learning outcomes, analyses of teacher-made tests have sometimes been suggested as an additional source of evaluative evidence. Although this evidence is usually labeled teacher-*made* tests, that is, teacher-constructed classroom assessments, the evidence might also include teacher-*selected* tests such as the tests a teacher adopts from those assessments supplied by textbook publishers or commercial testing firms.

Two factors in the appraisal of such tests are typically considered. For openers, an analysis by a teacher evaluator can reveal the extent to which a teacher's classroom assessments do, in fact, represent the skills and knowledge embodied in whatever official content standards are supposed to be the targets of that teacher's instruction. Often, those content standards will be whatever a state's education authorities have chosen as their state-approved curricular aims. But, of course, what's in a teacher's classroom tests (either in those tests created by the teacher or in any tests chosen or adapted from other sources) will not only mirror official content standards, but will frequently measure students' mastery of en route subskills and knowledge. These enabling subskills and knowledge can be regarded as "building blocks" leading to students' mastery of the more terminal, officially endorsed curricular targets. Analysts, of course, would need to be trained to know what to look for in determining the degree to which a teacher's tests are aligned with official content standards, and then helped regarding how to supply a succinct and accurate description of that alignment's quality.

Another focus of a scrutiny of teachers' classroom assessments could be to verify the level of curricular aspiration embodied therein. Often referred to these days as "depth of knowledge" (DOK), those who analyze teacher-made tests might focus on determining a test's DOK. They might be judging whether a teacher's classroom assessments measure students' mastery of higher-order curricular outcomes such as cognitive skills calling for evaluations and syntheses or, on the other hand, whether those assessments deal only with lower-order outcomes such as students' memorization of factual information. While some teachers might, if interviewed, claim that their instruction was targeted at truly challenging, high-aspiration DOK goals, an analysis of the tests those teachers employ to ascertain their students' learning could reveal that rarely, if ever, are students asked to come up with anything other than memories of trivial facts.

For these two missions, analyses of teacher-made tests can supply useful information. However, please note that these analyses only illuminate the nature of a teacher's *curricular* targets, not the *instructional* quality with which those targets have been pursued. Using our continuing example, if a teacher-evaluation process deals only with a teacher's *instructional ability*, then the analysis of teacher-made tests would not seem to be particularly relevant—unless those devising the teacher-evaluation system had decided that a teacher's instructional ability must, of necessity, embrace the teacher's curricular targets.

Teachers' Self-Ratings

Although some might claim that teachers should have an opportunity to contribute to any evaluation of their own capabilities by providing personal ratings as evidence of their own effectiveness, this is difficult to accept when the evaluation is to be summative in nature. On the other hand, when the thrust of a teacher evaluation is formative, it makes good sense for teachers, perhaps working with their school's principal or with other supervisors, to rate their own instructional strengths and weaknesses. Such weaknesses, once identified, perhaps collaboratively by a teacher working with a supervisor, can then be addressed so that those shortcomings can be overcome.

However, when the focus of a teacher-evaluation program is dominantly summative, even if—at a later point—a teacher who is in need of support can become the recipient of formatively oriented teacher evaluation, teachers' self-ratings have no legitimate role in such summative teacher evaluations.

AUGMENTATION OR OBFUSCATION?

Looking back at the 11 kinds of potential teacher-evaluation evidence considered in this chapter, those who design teacher-appraisal systems are faced with an immediate choice, namely, should they include or exclude certain of these evidence sources and, if they are to be included, how much evidential weight should they receive? Although, in the next chapter we will be recapping several particulars regarding how to implement a weighted-evidence judgmental approach to teacher evaluation, even before we get there it should be clear that this is another of those places when human judgment should govern the evaluative enterprise.

Teacher evaluators must decide whether the potential contribution of any of these evidence sources is worth the cost and trouble of garnering it. In this instance, *worth* should be determined by the increased accuracy of judgments regarding a teacher's quality. Clearly, some of the potential evidence sources treated here are less worthy than are others. Certain evidence-sources may contribute more, some less, to the appraisal of a specific teacher's ability. Some of the potential evidence sources treated in the chapter are apt to be worth the money and the hassle they will require. Some aren't. Moreover, there may be other kinds of evaluative evidence beyond those sundry sources treated in this chapter. The worth of those sources, too, should be judged according to a cost-effective determination regarding their likely contribution to a defensible evaluation of a specific teacher.

The more numerous the sources of evidence we use regarding a teacher's quality does not automatically translate into a stronger teacher-evaluation program than those programs relying on fewer sources of evidence. A weighted-evidence judgmental approach to teacher evaluation based on three or four truly incisive kinds of evidence will be better than a similar approach featuring many more sources of evidence, some of which are clearly tangential or only arguably relevant to determining a teacher's quality. As always, someone needs to make a judgment about whether additional sources of evidence actually improve teacher evaluations or, in fact, becloud such evaluations.

EVIDENTIAL-WEIGHT GUIDELINES

When deciding which, if any, of the sundry evidence sources treated here should receive an invitation to take part in a teacher-evaluation program, once more a *human judgment* chord is heard being strummed on this book's nearly incessant advocacy guitar. Sensible teacher evaluators will, as usual, need to judge whether each of these sources of evidence sufficiently illuminates a teacher's quality so that, surely in addition to other sources of evidence, it should be added to the teacher-evaluation evidence mix. If a particular evidence source is, in fact, included, then the following two guidelines should be considered:

- Greater evidential weight should be given to any source of cost-affordable evidence for which research or common sense suggests that such evidence can help us more accurately gauge a teacher's quality.
- Greater evidential weight should be assigned to evidence that has been competently collected in such a way that no obvious shortcomings in the evidence-gathering procedures are apt to distort the contribution of the evidence to an accurate evaluation of a teacher.

CHAPTER IMPLICATIONS FOR THREE AUDIENCES

For Policymakers: In a quest for multiple sources of evaluative evidence, officials in some states or districts may be inclined to incorporate a wide array of evidence-collecting procedures. Educational policymakers who consider the sorts of evidence treated in this chapter will surely conclude that many of them have no legitimate role in determining how effective a particular teacher actually is. This is where a "common-sense screen" can prove especially useful to those who ultimately establish the policies governing teacher-evaluation procedures. If the kind of evidence under consideration is affordable and can make a distinctive or corroborative contribution to the array of evidence being used to evaluate a teacher, then common sense suggests that such evidence should be included in what's used to judge teachers.

For Administrators: Depending on the degree to which local teacher evaluations can be customized at the district and/or school level, then the educational administrators who staff those schools and districts may wish to give serious attention to the sundry sources of evaluative evidence treated in the chapter. What was seen, more often than not, is that a type of evaluative evidence possibly touted by some proponents actually has little merit in the appraisal of a teacher's quality. On the other hand, a few of the miscellaneous sorts of evaluative evidence treated in the chapter, if supported by a knowledgeable educational administrator, might be added to a local teacher-evaluation process and, thereby, could strengthen the evaluative process.

For Teachers: As we saw with educational policymakers and administrators, one important feature of this chapter was its attempt to lay out a variety of different evidence sources, many of which should probably have no role at all in the evaluation of teachers. Teachers should also consider, perhaps briefly, the 11 varieties of evidence described in the chapter so that a teacher can decide which, if any, of those kinds of evidence should be supported by to-be-evaluated teachers.

CHAPTER 9

Mission Possible?

This short wrap-up chapter has two missions and one answer. First, it will attempt to provide a brief recapitulation of what's been addressed in the book's earlier chapters. Second, and without any embarrassment whatsoever, I'll be making a pitch for you to personally look into the quality of any teacher-evaluation system that you have anything to do with—or that has anything to do with you. Thereafter, if you decide the teacher-evaluation program you're looking at has deficits, then I'll offer some suggestions regarding how you might get those shortcomings repaired. Finally, in a concluding paragraph, I'll supply my personal answer to the question of whether America's current preoccupation with teacher evaluation is likely to pay off.

Now, because the chapter's initial, recapping mission will help set the table for its subsequent improvement mission, let's get underway with that reprise.

WEIGHTED-EVIDENCE
JUDGMENT OF TEACHERS: A REPRISE

The reason this book was written can be succinctly expressed. Because America's teachers are soon to be evaluated more rigorously than ever before, and because many of those teacher evaluations may be flawed, increased knowledge regarding the basics of teacher evaluation is needed by educational policymakers, educators, and other citizens—especially parents of school-age children. Because the way America's teachers are to be evaluated will influence how those teachers teach, the unsound evaluation of teachers is certain to have a negative impact on the schooling of our children. Accordingly, we dare not sit back passively if ill-conceived evaluations are imposed on the nation's teachers.

This brief book attempts to supply its readers with sufficient information so that, if they wish, they can arrive at a reasonably accurate judgment about the quality of any state, district, or school teacher-evaluation program—either a program that's recently been created or a program that's currently being built. And then, if that teacher-evaluation program contains meaningful mistakes, a reader can actually try to help remedy those mistakes.

Two recent federal initiatives, the Race to the Top Program and the ESEA Flexibility Program, now call for states to engage in more stringent teacher evaluation. These federal programs are, without argument, the catalysts underlying most states' serious revamping of their teacher-evaluation frameworks. In particular, federal insistence on the use of multiple kinds of evidence to appraise teachers—including reliance on student growth as a significant evaluative factor—has inclined some states to embrace the wrong kinds of student-growth evidence.

In many states, preliminary versions of new teacher-evaluation systems have already been fashioned, and some are soon to be used in evaluating a state's teachers. In other states, plans for new teacher-evaluation procedures are now being formulated. Considerable differences exist regarding the degree to which a state's teacher-evaluation framework encourages or allows local variations in the appraisal of a given state's teachers.

It was contended early on in the book that, because some of the multiple evidence sources now being employed to evaluate teachers are more significant than others, and that the significance of certain evidence may need to be adjusted when applied to the evaluation of a particular teacher in a particular instructional setting, human judgment must play a prominent role if teacher evaluation is ever to be defensible.

The approach to teacher evaluation recommended herein was *weighted-evidence judgment*. This teacher-appraisal strategy calls for teacher evaluators to assemble as much quality-relevant evidence as they realistically can acquire, and then weight the evaluative significance of each evidence source chosen. In some instances, adjustments in the evaluative weight of certain evidence may be necessary when applied to a specific teacher.

The judgments required in weighted-evidence teacher evaluation can be made by one or more teacher evaluators. A teacher evaluator might be a school principal who, all by himself or herself, functions as a solitary weighted-evidence judge. If more resources are available, teacher evaluators might be organized in small groups to form review panels. Whoever is carrying out a weighted-evidence judgmental evaluation of teachers should be given adequate training for this assignment—fundamentally different than teacher evaluations of the past.

A weighted-evidence approach to teacher evaluation will not be flaw-free. Mistakes will be made. Nonetheless, because this approach incorporates human judgment at key points in the evaluative process, fewer mistakes will be made than if a "people-proof" process were used that allows no variations in evidence weighting at the very moments when such weighting is pivotal.

It was also argued that while both *formative* (improvement-focused) teacher evaluation and *summative* (appraisal-focused) teacher evaluation should definitely be undertaken, those evaluations must be carried out separately—and definitely not using the same teacher evaluators.

In five consecutive chapters, the commonly employed sources of evidence for teacher evaluation were described along with recommendations regarding when to give those sources greater evidential weight. Particular concern was registered regarding states' heavy reliance on their annual accountability tests because those tests are rarely accompanied by evidence supporting their use in the evaluation of teachers' instructional skill.

Summing up, then, the approach to teacher evaluation advocated in this book represents a strategy in which evaluative judgments are made about a teacher's quality based on an initial weighting of diverse evidence and then adjusted, if necessary, when the evidence is applied to the evaluation of a particular teacher. It was contended that, if care is taken at all stages of teacher evaluation to maximize the objectivity and accuracy of the process, the resultant judgmental appraisals of teachers will be more accurate than those achieved by any evaluative strategy in which human judgment does not play a prominent role.

What to Do—and How?

What are you to do if you discover that a given teacher-evaluation program—already created or being built—appears to incorporate serious weaknesses? The remaining pages of this book will attempt to answer this key question. What follows will not be a sure-fire, step-by-step roadmap for improvement. That's because teacher-evaluation frameworks vary substantially from state to state—and are operated by individuals who possess diverse talents and points of view. An improvement prescription set forth for State A and implemented by State A personnel may flop when employed in State B and implemented by State B personnel. In teacher evaluation, as in all things, we need to match the tasks to the talent. Accordingly, what I'll try to lay out is a set of suggested actions that, if followed, are more likely to result in an improved teacher-evaluation program—most of the time. In a sense, the suggestions I'll be proffering represent my version of "likely payoff" principles, but in this instance the payoff is focused on shaping up what appears to be an inadequate teacher-evaluation program.

Please regard the bold-faced suggestions to follow as just that—suggestions. They are presented in roughly the order that most people might follow them, but there is nothing sacrosanct about the sequence in which these suggestions are given or in the need to carry out each and every one of them. All of the suggestions are predicated on the assumption that you have a meaningful interest in a teacher-evaluation program, one that's already in place or one that's currently being built. Perhaps you are a teacher who is soon to be evaluated. Or, possibly, you might be a parent who worries about the evaluation of the teachers in your own child's school. You might also be an educational policymaker, such as a local school board member, who is concerned about whether a state's teacher-evaluation framework is likely to enhance or diminish educational quality in the school district for which you are responsible. In short, you most likely are a member of one of the three audiences addressed with chapter implications at the close of each chapter, namely, policymakers, administrators, or teachers.

What I'm assuming is that you care about the way students will be taught as a consequence of the teacher-evaluation system in which you are interested. Well, if you care enough about that teacher-evaluation program to give it some serious attention, here are some suggestions I hope you'll consider. To keep the focus and phrasing of these suggestions constant, they will all be addressed to the same person—you.

Suggestion 1: Familiarize yourself with the most important issues faced by teacher evaluators.

Now here's a surprise—you've already followed this very first suggestion! That is, you've done so if you've seriously been reading this book. If so, you really have become conversant with the most significant issues associated with the evaluation of teachers. You've seen, for example, that although there is a widespread belief that classroom observation can provide an accurate estimate of a teacher's skill, this tends to be true for only the very best and the very worst teachers. For the huge group of mid-quality teachers, the evidence provided by classroom observations supplies much less evaluative precision than is usually thought.

Similarly, because of the federal government's insistence on incorporating student growth as a significant factor in the appraisal of a teacher, you've seen that reliance on instructionally *insensitive* tests, either state-administered standardized tests or teacher-built classroom tests, can lead to serious mistakes in appraising teachers. If a test measures what students bring to school rather than what those students are taught once they get there, then serious use of those tests' results to evaluate teachers is unsound.

Suggestion 2: Learn as much as you can about the teacher-evaluation program in which you are interested.

Unless an emerging teacher-evaluation program is so early in its development process that it is still unformed, written documents (or online descriptions) about a teacher-evaluation program will almost always be available. To illustrate, suppose you reside in a state where, in order to secure a Race to the Top grant, state officials have developed and installed a brand-new, statewide teacher-appraisal program. Information regarding that teacher-appraisal system can usually be found on your state department of education's official website. By using such a website, or by contacting someone from the state department of education, you should be able to obtain a description of the documents your state has submitted to federal officials in an effort to obtain the formidable dollars that federal authorities have made available to the states.

If your interest is in a state-level framework for teacher evaluation (one that's created to guide educators in local districts and schools), then you can usually rely on an Internet search engine to request information regarding your specific state's "teacher evaluation." If you are more interested in teacher evaluation in your very own school district, or even at a specific school, then a phone call (or, more likely, several phone calls) might be required to obtain appropriate descriptive materials. Be assured that, with appropriate effort, you should be able to obtain information about almost any teacher-appraisal program in which you are interested.

If you discover that, at least at the state level, your state's educational leaders have recently undertaken a major modification in their teacher-evaluation program because of a federal initiative such as the ESEA Flexibility Program, then it also makes sense for you to secure, once more via the Internet, information about the kinds of teacher-evaluation programs that have been specifically recommended by federal authorities. In many instances, a state's teacher-evaluation system, quite deliberately, mirrors whatever federal authorities want. In other cases, state officials attempt to do a bit of limit testing by subtly departing from federal preferences. You should learn, for certain, how much district or school latitude seems to be incorporated in the implementation of your own state's teacher-evaluation framework. Currently, a considerable amount of variability can be seen in the degree to which some states' local educators are being allowed to depart from rules that, in other states, must be unbendingly followed.

Here is the U.S. Department of Education's official website: www.ed.gov. By going to that site, and searching for either Race to the Top or the ESEA Flexibility Program, you'll be able to discover how either or both of those two initiatives have influenced what's contained in the teacher-evaluation program in which you are interested.

Suggestion 3: If you find serious deficits in a teacher-evaluation program, consider allying yourself with like-minded colleagues who might wish to remedy those problems.

Let's say you are interested in how your district-level teacher evaluations are going to take place and, after getting some fairly detailed information from your state department of education (or from the administrative office of your local school district), you conclude that both the state and your district seem to have done a top-flight job in constructing what appears to be a really sensible teacher-appraisal system. You don't find any serious weaknesses in what is being done with regard to teacher evaluation in the state or in your district. If that's the case, then count your blessings. There seems to be no need for further action. Turn your attention to other interests. Get a hobby.

However, as is far more likely, you may identify some serious shortcomings in what's being planned either at the state level or in the way your school district's officials are planning to implement the state's framework. For instance, suppose you learn that your district's leaders have unwisely jammed together the formative and summative functions of teacher evaluation so that neither the improvement mission nor the evaluation mission of the district's teacher-appraisal program seem well served. You conclude, in fact, that because of this contamination, along with other evaluative mistakes, many of your district's teachers are almost certain to be misevaluated.

At that point, then, because "squeaky wheels get greased," and because more people working on this sort of task can squeak more loudly than you can all by yourself, enlist the support of collaborators. If you are a parent, ask more parents to join you in what is clearly a constructively focused mission. If you are a district school board member, make sure that other members of your board—or members of other school boards—have a chance to join you in a serious effort to study and identify potential improvements for the teacher-evaluation system you're reviewing.

If your expanded group concurs with your analysis of the teacher-appraisal program's shortcomings, then decide together on the most effective method of getting a group-developed "repair-it" message into the hands of the most appropriate decision makers. Perhaps, if state-level weaknesses have been found, you will end up directing your concerns to your state's chief state school officer. Maybe you will want to communicate your identification of problems to your school district's superintendent or to the chair of your district's school board. You can, of course, do these things all by yourself. But it usually is more successful if you do it as part of an audibly squeaking team.

Influencing the "most appropriate decision makers" so that they take action to remedy identified deficits in a teacher-evaluation program (the one identified by you and your associates) is not fools' play. Influencing decision makers is a challenge. Over the years, I have found that the most potent way to motivate influential decision makers to endorse a needed improvement, for example, in any sort of educational accountability program, is to present a proposed modification so it is patently beneficial to the decision makers themselves. That's right; try to package a proposed change in a troubled teacher-evaluation program so that decision makers recognize that the resulting change will be in their *personal* best interest.

For instance, if the elected members of a state school board realize that if they can make their state's teacher-evaluation program more accurate, and thereby more fair to the state's teachers, not only will this change improve instruction in the state's schools, but the state's teachers will also be properly appreciative. Elected leaders rarely reject the opportunity to take credit for accomplishments! Candidly, it is not always easy to devise a proposed modification in a teacher-evaluation program so it benefits *both* education and the decision makers who must make the proposed change. But if you and your colleagues can come up with a way to do so, then there's a far better chance that you can get those in authority to remedy a teacher-evaluation system's shortcomings.

Suggestion 4: Don't be deferent—by assuming that "experts" have properly crafted a teacher-evaluation program.

The sad truth is that many of the U.S. teacher-evaluation programs devised during the last few years appear to be laden with shortcomings. Don't assume that experts with genuine teacher-evaluation savvy were waiting in the wings and, once called on because of federal initiatives, were able to devise sparkling teacher-appraisal programs for our states. On the contrary, America currently has a dearth of folks who know a whole lot about how to evaluate teachers. Let's face it, for many decades in America our public schools have embraced a decidedly soft teacher-evaluation culture. Rarely in years past, for example, have we seen substantial numbers of public school teachers "deselected" because of their instructional inadequacies. Yet, given the enormous numbers of teachers who staff our schools, it is surely the case that substantial numbers of ineffective teachers should have, after a proper evaluation, been forced to seek a career in which they could do less harm to children.

The sort of teacher evaluation now being called for by federal authorities is the exact opposite of soft. The kind of teacher-evaluation process being sought by Uncle Sam is a summative, not formative, appraisal of America's teachers. And it is supposed to be a more rigorous teacher-evaluation approach in which—to demonstrate that serious in-school learning is actually taking place—student growth must become a significant determiner of a teacher's quality. Few educational researchers have studied, researched, or even thought about this sort of tough-minded summative evaluation of teachers. You need to recognize that, at least for the next few years, many teacher-evaluation specialists won't be available.

Although the teacher-evaluation frameworks formulated recently in most states attempt to subscribe to what's sought by federal authorities, in many instances state personnel are being forced to *invent* what seem to be the best ways of doing what needs to be done. These state-level workers seem to be coping as well as they can with what, for most of them, are brand-new tasks. And, of course, early-on inventions—whatever the arena—often don't work as well as their inventors had hoped. Don't be astonished, therefore, if you encounter aspects of a teacher-evaluation program that seem flawed. They probably are.

After reading the previous eight chapters, you have acquired enough know-how so you can raise many significant questions of the individuals who have devised any state or local teacher-evaluation program. Toss your questions at the folks running that program, then listen to their answers. If their plans don't make *common sense,* then it is likely that those plans are not sensible.

Suggestion 5: Remember, because you are setting out to ensure that a teacher evaluation is not harmful to children, don't let up until you see a sound teacher-evaluation process in place.

It may seem like a stretch to imagine that just one person, *you,* might be able to bring about serious changes in the nature of a teacher-evaluation program that can have so much impact not only on teachers, but also on the students they teach. For the most part, the teacher-evaluation programs recently spawned by two federal initiatives were intended to have better teachers teaching our children. But because of rampant unfamiliarity with the summative evaluation of teaching, some serious mistakes are now apt to be made in how teachers are to be evaluated. Those mistakes can damage children educationally—and sometimes permanently. Something must be done to correct those mistakes. Perhaps you are the person to do that something.

These are not plush fiscal times for educators. State and local school officials are rarely worried about how best to spend a budget surplus. Accordingly, in thinking through how best to evaluate teachers, it will be important for you to support affordable and practicable alternatives to any existing teacher-appraisal program. Simply advocate the best evaluation procedures that, realistically, can be afforded.

CHAPTER IMPLICATIONS FOR THREE AUDIENCES

For Policymakers: The most important realization for educational policymakers may well be a recognition that in our nation's vast school systems we do not now possess teacher-evaluation strategies suitable for the task at hand—nor sufficient experts to create those evaluative strategies. That recognition should spur policymakers to view with warranted caution *any* teacher-evaluation procedures they encounter.

For Administrators: An educational administrator's success is, without question, dependent on the effectiveness of the teachers for whom that administrator is responsible. This chapter calls for readers to learn about the key issues in teacher evaluation, and to take an active role in improving any relevant teacher-evaluation program. In the case of district-level and school-site leaders, this translates to (1) learning about the nature of defensible judgment-based teacher evaluation, (2) determining whether a particular teacher-evaluation program is in need of fixing, and then (3) attempting to fix it in a cost-effective fashion.

For Teachers: Teacher evaluation, by definition, is designed to evaluate teachers. That being the case, especially as the consequences associated with today's new teacher-evaluation programs are increasing substantially, teachers really have no recourse except to learn as much as they can about how to evaluate teachers and then, if they are slated to be evaluated inappropriately by a deficient teacher-evaluation process, attempt to head off the mistakes most likely to be made.

RESPONDING TO A SUBTITLE

Earlier, I promised to answer the book's subtitle query before we ran out of pages. With pages running out, it's now or never. The question implied by the *Mission Possible?* subtitle is obvious, namely, can the recent surge of interest in evaluating U.S. teachers be carried out in a way that is not only fair to the teachers being evaluated, but also can improve the quality of education provided to the nation's students? Well, what follows is my personal, one-paragraph answer.

When federal policymakers called for the creation of state-level evaluative programs for teachers relying on multiple sources of evidence, the most significant of which was to be test-based evidence of students' learning, they did a very good thing. All professionals—including teachers—should be evaluated according to the consequences of their efforts. For the sake of America's children, we want our very best teachers to be staffing our schools. Accordingly, if the right sorts of evidence are assembled, given appropriate evaluative weights that can, if necessary, later be adjusted for particular teachers, the vast majority of our teachers can be accurately and fairly evaluated. If teachers are accurately evaluated, and given opportunities for needed improvements, then U.S. students will end up being better taught. But in order to employ the right evidence and to weight it properly, teacher evaluators will need to employ their very best judgments. Given the right evidence and the suitable weighting of that evidence, appropriately evaluating America's teachers is definitely possible. For the sake of the children those teachers teach, we need to make this possibility a reality.

References

Black, P., & Wiliam, D. (1998). Assessment and classroom learning. *Assessment in Education: Principles, Policy and Practice, 5*(1), 7–73.

Danielson, C. (1996). *Enhancing professional practice: A framework for teaching.* Alexandria, VA: Association for Supervision and Curriculum Development.

Danielson, C. (2007). *Enhancing professional practice: A framework for teaching* (2nd ed.). Alexandria, VA: Association for Supervision and Curriculum Development.

Danielson, C. (2011). *The framework for teaching evaluation instrument.* Princeton, NJ: The Danielson Group.

Heritage, M. (2013). *Formative assessment: A process of inquiry and action.* Cambridge, MA: Harvard Education Press.

Hess, F. M. (2012). Foreword to S. Mead, A. Rotherham, & R. Brown, The Hangover: Thinking about the unintended consequences of the nation's teacher evaluation binge. *Teacher Quality 2.0, Special Report 2.* Washington, DC: American Enterprise Institute.

Marzano, R. J. (2003). *What works in schools: Translating research into action.* Alexandria, VA: Association for Supervision and Curriculum Development.

Marzano, R. J. (2006). *Classroom assessment and grading that work.* Alexandria, VA: Association for Supervision and Curriculum Development.

Marzano, R. J. (2007). *The art and science of teaching: A comprehensive framework for effective instruction.* Alexandria, VA: Association for Supervision and Curriculum Development.

Marzano, R. J., Frontier, T., & Livingston, D. (2011). *Effective supervision: Supporting the art and science of teaching.* Alexandria, VA: ASCD.

Marzano, R. J., Pickering, D. J., & Marzano, J. S. (2003). *Classroom management that works: Research-based strategies for every teacher.* Alexandria, VA: Association for Supervision and Curriculum Development.

Marzano, R. J., Pickering, D. J., & Pollack, J. E. (2001). *Classroom instruction that works: Research-based strategies for increasing student achievement.* Alexandria, VA: Association for Supervision and Curriculum Development.

Marzano, R. J., & Waters, T. (2009). *District leadership that works: Striking the right balance.* Bloomington, IN: Solution Tree Press.

Marzano, R. J., Waters, T., & McNutty, B. A. (2005). *School leadership that works: From research to results.* Alexandria, VA: Association for Supervision and Curriculum Development.

McCune, G. (2012, October 4). *Chicago teacher union ratifies deal that ended strike.* Reuters.

McMillan, J. H. (2010). *Classroom assessment: Principles and practice for effective standards-based instruction* (5th ed.). Saddleback, NJ: Prentice-Hall.

Mead, S., Rotherham, A., & Brown, R. (2012). The hangover: Thinking about the unintended consequences of the nation's teacher evaluation binge. *Teacher Quality 2.0, Special Report 2.* Washington, DC: American Enterprise Institute.

Popham, W. J. (1988). The dysfunctional marriage of formative and summative teacher evaluation. *Journal of Personnel Evaluation in Education, 1*(3), 269–273.

Popham, W. J. (2008). *Transformative assessment.* Alexandria, VA: ASCD.

Popham, W. J. (2011). *Transformative assessment in action.* Alexandria, VA: ASCD.

Popham, W. J. (2014). *Classroom assessment: What teachers need to know* (7th ed.). Upper Saddle River, NJ: Pearson.

Popham, W. J., & Lindheim, E. (1981, September). Implications of a landmark ruling on Florida's minimum competency test. *Phi Delta Kappan, 63*(1), 18–22.

Popham, W. J., & Ryan, J. M. (2012). *Determining a high-stakes test's instructional sensitivity.* Paper presented at the annual meeting of the National Council on Educational Measurement, April 12–16, Vancouver, BC, Canada.

Rich, M. (2012, October 15). Seeking aid, school districts change teacher evaluations. *New York Times.* Retrieved from http://www.nytimes.com

Scriven, M. (1967). The methodology of evaluation. In R. E. Stake (Ed.), *Curriculum evaluation.* American Educational Research Association Monograph Series on Evaluation, No. 1, Chicago, IL: Rand McNally.

Stiggins, R. J., & Chappuis, J. (2012). *An introduction to student-involved assessment FOR learning* (6th ed.). Boston, MA: Pearson Education.

U.S. Department of Education. (2011). *ESEA flexibility.* Washington, DC: Author.

Wiliam, D. (2011). *Embedded formative assessment.* Bloomington, IN: Solution Tree.

Index

CORWIN

A SAGE Company

The Corwin logo—a raven striding across an open book—represents the union of courage and learning. Corwin is committed to improving education for all learners by publishing books and other professional development resources for those serving the field of PreK–12 education. By providing practical, hands-on materials, Corwin continues to carry out the promise of its motto: **"Helping Educators Do Their Work Better."**